GRANDparents' Corner

GRANDparents' Corner

Barbara Stephens

Hillsboro Press

PROVIDENCE PUBLISHING CORPORATION
FRANKLIN, TENNESSEE

Printed in the United States of America

08   07   06   05   04   1   2   3   4   5

Library of Congress Control Number: 2004114522

ISBN: 1-57736-330-2

Cover design by Hope Seth

Cover photograph by Lara Purcell

HILLSBORO PRESS
an imprint of
Providence Publishing Corporation
238 Seaboard Lane • Franklin, Tennessee 37067
www.providence-publishing.com
800-321-5692

To Kenny,
the love of my life.

Kenneth R. Stephens
1923–2002

"To live in hearts we leave, is not to die."
—T. Campbell

Contents

Preface

IN 1982, I WAS HIRED BY KNOX COUNTY SCHOOLS TO be a part-time adult education teacher. At that time I was sent into sites that needed basic skills or preparation for a general equivalency diploma. One of my first locations was the John T. O'Connor Senior Center in Knoxville, Tennessee.

The class had three older ladies who let me know their interest was in fractions and spelling only. For about five months, every Wednesday, we studied fractions and had spelling bees. They never did learn fractions and rarely approved of my selections of spelling words.

Feeling that I was banging my head against a wall, Director Ruth Peterson was very willing for me to try some other educational avenues. I invited a local, well-known meteorologist to come and talk about the weather. The center advertised this program and thirty-five people showed up for it. As these visitors introduced themselves, I quickly realized most of them were well-educated, retired seniors who were interested in learning about up-to-date technology, writing their memoirs, dealing with lifestyle changes, and discussing their various opinions of "this new generation."

Being fairly quick on my feet—as teachers must be—I announced that the following week we would be discussing genealogy and that an expert would be on hand to answer questions. I had no clue who I would find to be an expert, but I knew somebody could be found.

During my next week, I found the expert and created an interest survey about what this new group would like to discuss, which other specialists they would like to hear, and developed a list of various topics and hobbies.

Our second meeting with this fresh group prompted an innovative name for the class. They didn't want to be linked in with the "fraction and spelling" group. The group came up with "Real Life" and this quickly became *the* class to attend at the O'Connor Center.

The troupe grew and varied topics continued. Often we would discuss aging or some problems they had with their adult children or Grandchildren. One member presented a problem that would quickly face others.

"My divorced daughter announced she is spending the weekend in Gatlinburg with her new boyfriend. She expects me to baby-sit my nine-year-old Granddaughter while she goes off to do something I am highly against. What should I do?" (Remember this was in 1985!)

This question brought about a six-week study of modern-day Grandparenting. About the same time the *Knoxville News-Sentinel* was beginning a section titled "50 Plus." The editor of this segment had asked if I would do a column for this once-a-month edition. I pitched him the Grandparenting Q&A idea. He was all for it, but noted that I would need to have a title.

I took this matter to the Real Life class, since they would basically be answering the questions. After much discussion, but with 100 percent agreement, they declared the column would be titled "Grandparents' Corner."

The rest is history!

In 1997, the Nashville *Tennessean* contacted me to see if we could work out a weekly column. The *Sentinel* later dropped my monthly column, but the *Tennessean* and I continued a wonderful relationship through August 2003.

During this time many of my readers suggested that I compile some of the columns. So here it is! Enjoy!

Barbara S. Stephens

Author's note: Being an English teacher and a follower of the *Chicago Manual of Style* for book standards, I have always tried to comply with the rules. In *my* book, with the approval of Hillsboro Press, I see the necessity of capitalizing anything to do with GRAND. Grandparent is an important title. A Grandchild is an important person. So for those of you who might question my usage I understand, but I feel it is too vital a word to be minimized.

Acknowledgments

THE NUMBER OF PEOPLE TO THANK WOULD MAKE UP an entire book, but for this time, I want to give credit to a select team.

To my family: Steve and Cindy—for their love and never-ending patience. Tod and Loretta—for their encouragement, prayers, and inspiration. Barbara Elizabeth, a wonderful stepdaughter, a best friend, and a steadfast presence of her Daddy's spirit. Chipper and Donna—for their continued devotion in watching over me.

To those fabulous Grandchildren who provide insight, encouragement, laughter, answers, and straightforward love. I promise to never reveal the secrets you share with only me: Stephen, Sean, Tyler, Paul, Amanda, Jessica, Hayden, and Audrey.

To Carolyn, from the beginning to the end, never failing, never faltering, always there for Kenny, for me—the assurance that our friendship will hold up through any kind of trials and tribulations. To Renae, for being a second mother to Dolly and Benson, hiking with me through parts unknown, buying milkshakes when the mood turns blue, and a top-notch Grandmother. To Lynn, a special friend who keeps me coherent by controlling the insane troll who inhabits my computer. To my prayer partners, Regina, Ann Mc, Nancy, Eleanor, Ann W., and Juanita, who manage to make life simple by carrying my burdens and sharing the joy.

To the *Knoxville News-Sentinel* and the Nashville *Tennessean* for providing the media to pursue my dream.

To my Lord and Savior for all good and perfect gifts.

GRANDparents' Corner

Chapter 1

MIXED EMOTIONS

Old Rules Need to Change
(Grandparenting Is No Longer the Same)

DID YOU KNOW THAT, ACCORDING TO THE ROPER Research Survey Group, 1999, every day in the United States six million people become Grandparents?

Many are excited, others are confused, thousands will tell you they have a great many concerns, but when all is said and done, most will agree that it is much easier than having children!

They question what their purpose will be in becoming a Grandparent. If you ask most Grandchildren, they will tell you that liking and loving is their idea of our role. Listening comes in a close second! Encouragement of their dreams and goals should also be a major direction for our energies.

Then we all wonder how our role will change with the parents. In order to keep up the good relationship with parents, considering our relationship with Grandchildren, we must be willing to meet the parents on their own terms. We should not have to change our values, but adjust our attitudes to their parenting rules. Their regulations may not suit you, but remember when you were the parent?

Then there is always that gigantic debate on gift-giving. Most of us are guilty of rushing out to buy stuff, but we do not want our little ones to look in the Grandparenting view-finder and only see *things*! One of the most important gifts we can give our Grandchildren is a recorded history of their family. Start with pictures and stories about their parents and work back through the family tree.

Being a role model is usually what Grandparents say they want to be for their Grandchildren. If they see us pay the *true* price of admission to a movie or the zoo, they remember! If we calmly and quietly handle the driver that almost hit us, they remember! If we are always honest with them and keep their confidences, they will remember!

Helping our Grandchildren to be happy and positive is one of this new generation's difficulties. Today's children see and hear so much that is negative, it might be up to us to keep their lives going in an up-beat direction. Happiness is contagious. Teach them to whistle. Show them that this world is a wonderful place to live. Make sure you are living your own life to the fullest.

Now go out there and enjoy your new title of *Grandparent.*

Q: Help! I just found out I am going to be a Grandmother and I am only forty-five! I am too young and busy for this. How do other people handle this traumatic news?
Sylvia, Chattanooga

Dear Sylvia,

I hope you have very fond memories of your Grandmother, but if she was anything like mine she wore shiny, high-top shoes, long, dark print dresses, and kept her gray hair pulled back in a bun. She sat most of the day in a rocking chair and quilted or made rag rugs.

Today's Grandmother works away from home (maybe even owns a business); bowls two nights a week; goes camping or hang gliding on the weekend; and looks like Priscilla Presley (also a Grandmother). Most of us work and make our own spending money. We have both the energy and the nerve to go white-water rafting with our Grandchildren. We go to aerobic classes and revel in the compliments when a six-year-old says, "You don't look like a Grandma!"

Times have changed and you are fortunate enough to be a vivacious part of that transformation.

Whoopi Goldberg is a Grandmother—does she fit the image? Watch Raquel Welch and hope that you, too, can fit into the modern-day version of "Granny."

Q: I am a new Grandparent and I am afraid that I am not going to be good at this. Do you have any hints that might help or make me feel better?
Chris, Murfreesboro

Dear Chris,

One of my favorite quotes from Alex Haley always makes me feel more confident as a Grandparent: "No one on earth can do for little children what Grandparents do. Grandparents tend to sprinkle stardust on young lives that binds and stretches—binds in love, and stretches their growth and experience."

That sounds simple enough. The ability to love Grandchildren seems to come natural to most of us—partly because we don't feel the pressure of rearing them.

A Grandparent who loves a child completely, unconditionally, and without reproof frees that child to love you with the same simplicity.

Q: All I hear from my friends who have Grandchildren are how great and wonderful this experience can be. I am still not sure about it. It just sounds like another step to growing older and doing it quicker. Do you want to convince me otherwise?

Not Sure, Franklin

Dear Not Sure,

My opinion is that Grandchildren bring out the extraordinary in all of us. We have talents and passions that may have become lost in the shuffle of raising our families. Grandchildren seem to have a unique way of prowling around in our inner self and finding that lost dream.

I think you will find that Grandparenting is much easier than being a parent. I loved my sons, but I was continually tense and concerned that I wasn't doing everything correctly. With Grandchildren, almost anything we do is fun and suitable.

Grandparents can wear almost anything we want and the little ones think it is awesome. Our eight-year-old Granddaughter was watching me debate what to wear to a party. "Whichever you choose will still look like you and that is good," she diplomatically reflected.

Grandparents have the advantage of living more than one life—through the eyes and legs of Grandchildren. Some of us may not be able to compete athletically, but we can enjoy watching *them* do it! I readily admit that I cannot play computer games but am so thrilled to have Grandchildren with the intelligence and nimble fingers to compete with the best.

Grandparents can have a "terrible, awful, no-good day" and have it completely erased by two tiny, soft arms around the neck and a whisper of "I wuv you."

Grandparents may feel that life is rushing by too quickly, but this does enable us to see a Grandchild abruptly become a maturing adult. It seems only yesterday we were rocking and singing to those who are now graduating from college.

We have a different neighbor. Oh, her name is the same and she still looks identical, but she is a *new* Grandmother—and what a change! I now hear a softer voice when she talks of baby-sitting six-month-old Austin and notice a new sparkle when she sees the parents' car turn into our street.

Oh yes, Grandparenting can do marvelous reconstruction to our mind and soul.

Q: I am having a difficult time trying to decide what my Grandchildren expect of me. One day they seem to want a Granny who will sit with them, read books, and bake cookies. The next day I feel they are expecting me to go out and conquer the local theme park in one hour—rides and all! I hear them talk about other Grandmothers and their work: "Casey's Nana is not old. She is a nurse!"

It sounds as if they think my staying home makes me ancient. I'm not aged, but I feel a need to settle in to some quiet time with my Grandchildren.

Martha, Harriman

Dear Martha,

Grandparenting today can be confusing—both for us *and* the young people. One of our teenage Grandsons really upset me a few years ago as I was talking about wanting to see the movie *Lethal Weapon*. He quietly replied, "You would probably like *On Golden Pond* better." I went to see *Lethal Weapon* and refuse to this day to see *On Golden Pond*!

Grandchildren, like our own children, expect different roles on different days. Each Grandchild has a unique personality and that affects how they want us to be. After I took our nine-year-old Amanda to see the movie *Beethoven*, she indignantly reported back to her parents, "She laughed the whole time and everyone around was staring at her!" She also knows she can mess up my kitchen with her cooking and loves me anyway.

The joy of Grandparenting today is that we can be who we want to be. We should have learned that after many years of being responsible to assorted people, we can now lean back and do what we truly want to do.

There are weekends I wouldn't want to baby-sit for any of them. I would much rather be camping in the Smokies, shopping the malls, or merely daydreaming with hubby. Then there are days I want to provide a respite from parenting for our children, a time for me to share my energy with excitable youngsters. They give me the opportunity to pretend I am twelve years old again.

Relax and be yourself. Your Grandchildren will love you for any variety of cheerful personalities you choose.

Q: *We have a new Grandson. He is our first and my role is unclear. I know I am not the parent. I can't always be there to meet the demands of little Tyson, and I don't want to be just a baby-sitter.*

Many of our friends say, "You now have more pleasures and less worry. You can spoil them and send them home."

It is such an exciting experience, and yet I am so afraid for the future of all young people. What is going to happen to this generation? Where do I fit in?

Confused in Oak Ridge

Dear Confused Grandmother,

I try not to worry about the future. I do well to manage one day at a time. By painful experience, I have learned three rules:

1. Be careful with sharing your wisdom. You have learned many of the pitfalls, but no one wants to hear about them. This causes more conflicts than any other component in family relations.

   If you feel you absolutely have to give advice, try not to do it too often. They may actually stuff a diaper in your mouth.

Many suggestions often conflict with the "in-laws" on the other side. Big Trouble!

2. Recognize that your baby now has one of his/her own. It is now his/her responsibility to play the adult role. Treat your child as a mature individual, no matter what you think!

3. Help your children realize your role has changed from the ever-present, devoted mother to an adult with life and work of your own.

Some children want their parents to continue the hovering in order for you to help with the child-rearing. Don't get caught in this trap. For the first time in many women's lives, we have the freedom to pursue our dreams, and we should value and guard our time adamantly.

On the other side of the coin, time with Grandchildren should be a big event. A time of pleasure and excitement—a time for racing back to your childhood and playing with Barbie dolls and Tonka toys again.

I had forgotten how much fun I had playing "dress up" until Amanda and Jessica came along.

Q: I am trying to be a good role model for my Grandchildren, but the task is not easy with television and movies ranting all the obscenity and garbage in young people's faces. I know their parents are trying to teach them right from wrong, but the pressure seems to come from outside the home. Do you have any ideas on what I can do as a Grandparent?

Charlie, Brentwood

Dear Charlie,

Wouldn't it be wonderful if there was a quick fix to this disgusting trend? When I was ten and picked up the word "gad" at camp, my mother warned me once and grounded me the second time. "That isn't a bad word," I defended. "It's close enough!" she countered.

One of my sons still talks of the time she overheard him use a no-no word and actually washed his mouth out with soap. Her philosophy was simple: "Only people who have a limited vocabulary use trash language and you are too intelligent for that!"

Oh, if it were that straightforward today.

A few mothers in the Knoxville area complained to the local NBC channel about the *Jerry Springer* show scheduled for the after-school crowd. They said it was too convenient for youngsters to come home unsupervised and watch his offensive material. The directors at the station gave in to the forceful parents and moved him to a morning slot.

I was inspired by this group of women and feel more of us can do something about eliminating or decreasing the amount of question-able material on TV. I am continually amazed at the number of parents who take their children to PG-13 movies. For those of you who haven't seen any of this level movies lately, there are no words that are unacceptable and the material is often adult humor.

Maybe I am living in a fantasy world, but I still feel there are more good kids out there today than those who talk trash. I want to believe that parents and Grandparents are a great influence on how our children speak and think. I want to believe that this negative trend will go away if we continue to object.

Q: *My husband and I took early retirement and are now expecting our first Grandchild. I can't bear the thought of this tiny baby in daycare. We are thinking of taking care of the baby, at least for a short time. We haven't mentioned this to our daughter. Is this a good idea?*

New Granny, Tullahoma

Dear New Granny,

My theory on Grandparenting and retirement is to "do what feels good." If this is something you and your husband agree on and your daughter is in favor of the situation, I see nothing unacceptable with this idea.

Some of your friends will probably think you are crazy for taking on this responsibility. Some will be jealous of the opportunity. Others will begin to relate the hazardous pitfalls. Don't listen to any of them.

You and your husband should sit down with your daughter and her husband and make some ground rules. Set up expectations of what you all agree. Discuss possible conflicts. Encourage weekly revisions or additional plans.

If you want to make sure you still have some time for yourself, be sure and set up a time line and allow no additional baby-sitting other than the agreed hours.

Are there other Grandparents involved? What will their feelings be? If they live out of town, there will probably not be a problem. If they live in town, you might want to include them in this planning discussion. Good relationship between Grandparents is always a good thing!

Q: It seems that many of the images of Grandparenting have to do with the Grandmothers. I hear so much about cookie-baking and girl stuff. Why do people assume that we Grandfathers cannot do an equal job of Grandparenting?

Grandparenting is not just woman's work. It is for everyone who loves their children. Grandfathers are just as interested in what is going on at school and in their social development as the Grandmothers.

Grandfathers are very capable of baby-sitting. Do they think we have never changed a diaper or made a snack?

Grandfathers are not as judgmental about change as people seem to think. I don't like earrings in odd places on either sex, but I can keep quiet.

I want to take a stand for Grandfathers and demand that we get some respect! We are a united group and demand equal privileges! Bring on the challenges!

Bill, Nashville

Dear Bill,

I am all for you campaigning to promote a stronger union for Grandfathers. I suggest you organize and meet on Monday afternoons at a local soccer field. After the game take all the Grandchildren out for pizza and return them home in time for homework.

First agenda meeting: Decide what traditions you want to pass on to your Grandchildren. Are these male traditions or attitudes that will help to overcome gender stereotypes? Will these customs promote opportunity for boys *and* girls to become more independent and self-sufficient?

Second agenda: What kind of difference do you want to make in a Grandchild's life? Expecting to be a good Grandparent and actually *working* at being one can be two different things.

In this busy time, we (men and women) need to be planning our course of action with our Grandchildren. Besides establishing traditions, we might want to visualize our own concept of the ideal Grandparent. What are we doing to exemplify that model? How can we begin to portray that person? What are our Grandchildren's emotional needs? How can we fulfill their insecurities?

Margaret Mead was quoted as saying, "You can be anything you set out to be, but first you must set out."

Q: As a Grandfather of three (ages twelve, ten, and seven), I think often of our role in the lives of these children.

It will not be easy for my Grandchildren to live up to the standards I would establish for them. The world they are growing up in is far different from the world I grew up in during the 1950s when smoking rabbit tobacco cigarettes was one of the things kids did to misbehave. Later, as teenagers we would occasionally raid a farmer's watermelon patch for a big, ripe melon. We were fearless.

My Grandchildren will not worry about imitation cigarettes and watermelons. The temptations they will face are far more dangerous. They must learn about alcohol and illegal drugs. They will face temptations of early sexual activity and the dangers of AIDS. They will learn that the consequences of these temptations are far more serious than those we faced.

The role of Grandparents is very different from that of my parents. It may be a less obvious role, but it is very important.

I want my Grandchildren to see me being the kind of person I hope they will want to be. If I am to expect them to be generous and considerate, then they will have to see me being generous and considerate of others. I cannot hope for them to have lives of integrity unless they can see that I am that kind of person. Children are fantastic observers and their memories are crystal clear. The attitude of "do as I say, not as I do" simply will not work in today's world.

I want their lives to be full and productive, both for themselves and for society. I hope they will be generous, kind, understanding, and respectful of others. I hope they will maintain a high level of integrity and live moral lives. Finally, I hope they will find something worthy and productive to do which will make a difference in the world.

I am still learning. Any advice?

Eddie C., Lebanon

Dear Eddie,

I think you have the basics down to a perfect model. Just keep doing what you are doing and sharing the non-judgmental love that only Grandparents can display.

Q: I am a Grandmother of three. I enjoy these wonderful blessings, but why don't I feel like a Grandmother?

My own Grandmother was a woman full of love, cookies, and all the time in the world to listen to my ramblings. I can't remember her ever talking about stress or a lack of time. Her world was leisurely paced and a very enjoyable time of life.

What happened? When will I ever get to be like that?

Evelyn, Columbia

Dear Evelyn,

Grandparents of today do not have the balance in their lives that our ancestors seem to have had. The simplicity has turned to complex scheduling.

Make an hourly list of what you do every day of every week, then notice how little time you spend watching birds or daydreaming.

We get so wrapped up in the trivial garbage; we forget how many hours are spent wasting precious time. According to a health study out of Wisconsin, we spend eight months of our lives opening junk mail. That is 5,760 hours of non-essential actions.

We have spent 8,640 hours looking for misplaced objects and, as we get older, those hours add up faster.

We have spent 17,280 hours trying to call people who are not home or whose phone is busy.

We are all so stressed out that many of us make no attempt to slow down, unless our bodies do the stopping for us. Balance comes when we make the time to discover ourselves and predetermine our priorities.

My mother would pick me up from school two or three afternoons a week and we would drive eight miles to visit my maternal Grandmother. If it was warm weather, she was always sitting in her glider when we arrived. She wasn't lazy, just had her work done and was getting in touch with herself—at least that is how I see it today.

To play the devil's advocate, let's assume that we can get our lives as balanced as our Grandparents did. How many Grandchildren and their mothers have three afternoons a week to come and swing on our porch? Talk about schedules! The balance must be for *your* own satisfaction.

Q: My only daughter has just found out that she is pregnant. She doesn't want me to come and help out when the baby is born. I have two sons and both of their wives let their mothers come and help at the birth of my other Grandchildren.

I am going to miss this experience because she is so stubborn and independent. She lives in Atlanta and I would have to make arrangements to take off from work, but I can easily do that.

What can I do or say to her. Why is she acting this way?

Sarah, Waverly

Dear Sarah,

I don't know why she is acting this way, but you aren't the only Grandmother to be turned down. I was also!

I was so excited at the prospect of my first biological Grandchild coming into the world with my loving and caring arms being the first one to do all those special little chores—first bath, first all-night awake! Since my daughter-in-law's mother had a small child to take care of, I offered the benefits of my wisdom.

"Thanks, Mom, but we are going to manage this production by ourselves. We feel it will be finer for the baby if we all bond together early. Maybe you can come later and spend a weekend," responded my fatherly-sounding son.

Well, I pouted quietly. I talked to myself in abundance about how greatly they would miss me. I felt sorry for myself. I prompted myself on how little they knew about babies. I lamented about missed opportunities. I whined a great deal in silence. You would have thought I had missed the chance to be Mrs. America!

After nine months of carrying my Granddaughter, my daughter-in-law called and in a suspiciously quiet voice asked, "Can you come when the baby is born? I'm not sure I can manage all there will be to do."

Delighted! Ecstatic! What a wonderful experience I was going to share with my new Granddaughter.

The episode wasn't as melodramatic as I had envisioned. Instead of playing new Granny, I cleaned house, cooked, washed clothes, and mowed their yard. Mommy and Daddy gave her the first bath and, thankfully, stayed up all night with the first case of tummy ache and changed all those baby-diarrhea diapers.

Being there was a wonderful experience. After the new wore off, I had all the rocking and loving I could manage.

You need to be patient with your daughter. This is an exciting time for her and it may be the occasion for her to say, "I can do this by myself."

Try to recall your first days as a new mom. You and your husband began a new journey that week. Remember the thrills, the joys, and the total unbelief at what you had created?

You will have plenty of opportunities to help out and be Grandma. Support her decision, but subtly remind her occasionally that you are available if she changes her mind.

Q: This Grandparenting job is not always easy. I am finding myself enjoying one of my Grandchildren much more than the rest. I know you are going to tell me that I can't do that! I also find that I dread two of them even talking about coming over to visit.

I am tired of being a working mother, Grandmother, and wife. Where do you get off talking about the joys of Grandparenting? I bet you have a maid and do not have a real job. You would feel different if you had to help raise part of your Grandchildren.

Disgusted, Clarksville

Dear Disgusted,

I detect a lot of frustration in your letter. I do have a *real* job. I do *not* have a maid. I clean my own toilets, and there are times I, also, feel there is no joy in Grandparenting. But then I get rested. The commotion slows down and I begin to see some daylight in my world.

Those parents (I suspect that includes you) who are rearing Grandchildren deserve a tribute the rest of us can never obtain. I have two cousins raising their Grandchildren and nothing I ever do will give me a seat higher in heaven than they have already attained.

Most Grandparents do have the privilege of sending the little ones home when they get rowdy, and we have the right to discipline them when they are in our own house.

Yes, most of us do have favorites. I have favorite friends, favorite cousins, and even favorite Grandchildren. But I hope they all think it is them!

I suspect you are having a rough time and need to be finding a few extra minutes for yourself. I won't presume to tell you how to find that time, but we all have the same number of hours in a day. Christian Bovee says, "Tranquil pleasures last the longest, for we are not capable of bearing great joys!" A tiny bit of diversion each day should improve your life.

Q: In a period of eighteen months, my three children gave me three wonderful Grandchildren. I was excited and promised myself I would be the perfect Granny. When they were small and cuddly, I loved them, dreamed of their futures, and gave myself to them equally. They are now middle-school age and I find that I "like" one of them better than the others. I feel terrible!

I try not to make a difference in the amount of time I spend with them, but I sure do look forward more to visits with my secret favorite. What am I going to do?

Imperfect Granny, Farragut

Dear Granny,

I called several of my Granny friends with your questions. If it will make you feel better, most of them have similar problems.

"Puppies and babies are all cute, but then they grow up," says one speaking anonymously. "I love all of my Grandchildren, but some have more appealing personalities."

A lot of it has to do with your own disposition. If you are outgoing you are going to find yourself more drawn to the ones who display the same characteristics. Activities that keep you both busy will energize you and create a feeling of oneness.

Quiet, calm children delight those of us who enjoy tranquil periods of togetherness. We can read, talk, listen at our own pace; not the frenzied state that appeal to some youngsters.

Try to enjoy time with each one and remember that "love" means more than the pleasure of togetherness.

Another friend told about one of her Granddaughters asking, "Am I your favorite Grandchild?" With much apprehension, the Grandmother replied, "What do you think?"

Little Miss Diplomat smiled smugly and whispered, "I know I am, but I'm not going to tell!"

As someone once said, "Let us prefer, but never exclude," seems to fix your quandary. Spending time with each individually will give you more insight into the other two's unique demeanor.

As long as no one knows who your preferred companion is, don't worry about it. Their personalities will change and your allegiance may shift often during the next decades. All Grandchildren are lovable—at one time or another!

Q: *I have ten Grandchildren, two stepGrandchildren, and two stepgreat-Grandchildren. I thought you might be interested in the job description they gave me.*

GRANDMOTHERS WANTED

* Lifetime position with responsibility for happiness, growth, and development of Grandchildren from birth to beyond maturity

* Work under supervision of directors of family-oriented organization anticipating expansion. Not an 8 to 5 job. May be some travel.

* Higher education not required, but previous experience as pediatrician helpful. Must have extensive knowledge of human relations.

* Computer experience not necessary. In five years, Grandchild will provide training. Skill in reading aloud essential.

* Successful applicant will have multiple duties and functions; caregiver/nurturer, playmate, wizard, teacher/mentor/historian, spiritual guide, and cheerleader.

* Individual must be loving, caring, loving, selfless, loving, accepting, and loving.

* Salary: Seven figures ($0,000,000) annually. Fringe benefits include overnight accommodations, in addition to generous amounts of hugs and kisses.

Now, what do you think of my want ad?

Clarice Orr, Lincoln, Nebraska

Dear Clarice,

Thank you so much for sending your job description. This gives me an idea on what to reply on those forms that ask, "What is your occupation?"

I may feel like a nurturer/caregiver, but when Grampa Kenny mentions going to the garden or feeding the birds, I lose my little darlings.

Grampa Kenny is also the historian, as he keeps them hypnotized with stories of great-great-Grandfather Shadrack Stephens.

They never call me to talk about track meets or football scores . . . but I'm the one they call to make school costumes.

Where could we find a part-time job that gives so much pleasure and requires so little training? There is not a book or class available that teaches people how to love a child, who comes equipped with a sparkle of joy and adoration in their eyes for the payoff.

A cross-stitch picture on our bedroom wall reads, "We shape our lives not by what we carry with us, but what we leave behind." I hope my children and Grandchildren will remember me for the love they see in my eyes, the caring in my voice, and the warmth of my hugs.

We are all very fortunate to serve many purposes to young people.

PARENTS' THOUGHTS

Q: I have a six-month-old daughter. She is the first Grandchild for my mother. She lives twenty-five hundred miles away and was only able to visit us last week. I was very disappointed in her reaction. She spent very little time at our house, because she was shopping and sight-seeing.

I had thought she would want to do all the Grandmotherly things, like giving her a bath, changing her clothes, feeding her, etc. She paid very little attention. She did bring back lots of clothes and toys from her shopping, but I would rather have had her attention. I had so many questions I wanted to ask, but never had the opportunity.

I can't get over the feeling that she doesn't want to be a Grandmother. Is there anything I can say to let her know about my feelings?

Disappointed New Mom, (e-mail)

Dear New Mom,

You didn't tell me the age of your mother. She may still be tired from raising children of her own. This is a common attitude of the youthfulness of some Grandmothers. If she still has children at home, she may not be ready to deal with another little one. She may not want to face the fact that she is old enough or you are old enough to have children.

You may be expecting her to be something she was never able to be for you. Becoming a Grandmother doesn't automatically make someone loving and mushy.

I have heard many young Grandmothers say, "Just about the time I had my life organized and was ready to do some things for myself, my daughter/son had a baby. I wish their timing had been different."

Keep her posted on your daughter's progress. Send her pictures and allow her to have some time to adjust to the new role she has been given. This new joy often unfolds like a flower. Sometimes it takes time to see the difference in parenting and Grandparenting.

Write or call and ask for advice. This is a great morale booster for Grandparents. They truly enjoy sharing their years of wisdom.

Be patient. Some Grandparents do better with toddlers than newborn babies. Some of us even like them better when they can talk.

Q: *I am pregnant with my mother's first Grandchild. I really want to be able to go visit my parents frequently after the baby comes (we see them three to four times a year) and I am sure she wants us to, because my parents are already talking about building a bigger house with a nursery.*

The problem is there are a couple of ideas that my mother has about child raising that make me really nervous about leaving the baby with her and visiting may not even be pleasant.

My mother thinks that children, even very young children, should be given credit for being intelligent and that, therefore, you should not child-proof the house at all. I remember that my sister and I grew up that way and everything worked out fine. I personally think it was more due to luck than that being a fabulous technique for raising children.

I don't think spanking is a great idea, but her idea is to spank the child after the fact every time they do something wrong. What we are dealing with is a safety issue (child is riding trike into street from driveway) and spanking afterwards.

Is it safe for me to leave my child with her, after she has told me she is not going to use cabinet locks or keep poisons and other dangerous items out of reach when we are there? Please help!

Apprehensive in Tullahoma

Dear Apprehensive,

A Grandmother who thinks babies are born knowing the rules and yet insists on punishing them if they disregard safety issues sounds as if she is looking for an argument.

This is your child and you are responsible. Even puppies need to know their boundaries and what is hazardous. Someone dependable must be with this child at all times and that may mean you—until the youngster fully understands responsibility.

I suppose she believes in letting someone stick their hand in the fire first in order to understand heat. Hopefully when the tiny baby arrives, your mother will soften her edges and adhere to your sensibility and rules.

Buy a baby book and share it with Granny.

Q: What do you call Grandparents who just cannot seem to make the time for their Grandchildren? My husband's parents are in their early sixties, are both employed (because they want to be), and they get away at their vacation home every weekend.

They won't change their weekend plans even if it is a Grandchild's birthday, but they will to attend a friend's party. They have never had a child-friendly house to go to—no special food (our children are all under the age of five) and definitely nothing to play with—not even a coloring book.

We live a short distance from them and they have visited our house three times in three years. When we do see them they are wonderful and fun to be with, and they act like they love our kids dearly. They don't even seem to be put off by having the children around.

My children clearly favor my parents who live in another state. They make certain to call my children on the phone at least two times a week and we visit them or they visit us three or four times a year.

I hate for my children to grow up feeling that their other Grandparents have no time for them. Am I crazy?

Bewildered, (e-mail)

Dear Bewildered,

Grandparents are like everyone else; individualistic and reactive in various ways. Your in-laws sound like the group that is not quite ready to settle in to the role you have envisioned for them.

They work, socialize, and live as if they are still enjoying the adventures of an empty nest. They may never bake cookies, have coloring books, or be the stereotypical Grandparents, but they "act like they love" your kids.

Do their friends have Grandchildren? Probably not. One of these days they will find themselves surrounded by other Grandparents and will want to share some of the same experiences they are all talking about.

In the meantime, enjoy the relationship you have with them. Many young people would be pleased to have their in-laws "fun to be around."

Even though your parents don't live near, continue that traditional relationship and be thankful for each day's blessings.

Children often experience hurt through their parents' eyes, but it is not necessarily something they would have noticed themselves.

GRANDPARENTS TO CARRY ON LEGEND

Q: Fond memories of my Grandparents compel me to describe the understanding older people in my life.

Although my paternal Grandfather died shortly before my birth, I was fortunate to have my maternal Grandfather until I was six years old.

I learned much about love sitting by the fireplace in his lap, as he patiently pulled sugar cane to satisfy my appetite for the cane's drippy sweetness.

But my younger sister, brother, and I were especially blessed with our two Grandmothers who lived with us most of our lives.

Mother worked, so these two women—very different, but alike in their devotion to us—virtually raised us. They cleaned house, cooked, washed, and still had time to shower us with love and special favors. I learned much that I know of the practical and philosophical aspects of life from them. Money could not buy the experience.

I might add that in all the years we lived together, I never heard one cross word between the three adult females in our family.

Sara Manis (author of Traveling with Mama), *Jamestown*

Dear Sara,

I often hear stories like yours of three adult females tending the house. My friend Norma told of her experience with her own mother and mother-in-law. One was recently widowed and the other one was ill and could no longer live alone. She and her husband, George, took both of them in and she said, "The two of them got along beautifully.

I didn't always have it so easy; trying to work and raise a small child, but everyone else seemed to enjoy themselves."

I admire families who can live together and share the benefit of so much wisdom. You and your siblings were left with a wealth of memories and love.

I was fortunate in having three Grandparents living nearby when I was growing up. I often remember those days of sitting under a huge oak tree, feeling the cool metal of their squeaky glider on my skinny, bare legs, and having lots of time to sit and listen while they told stories of their young courting days.

Grandparents of today are a new generation—active and busy. But I hope our Grandchildren will remember us as being filled to the brim with love, immeasurable understanding, and kindness.

Q: *I recently heard a young person complaining about her Grandfather. She said, "He is always grumbling about something I am doing or not doing. He always talks about his aches and pains and never seems happy."*

That touched a nerve with me. She made me wonder if that was how any of my Grandchildren feel. I certainly did not want to be described with those words, and yet I had heard myself voicing those phrases and grumbling about the joints, etc.

I have made an effort to stop griping about other's actions, to never mention my twinges or my medication, and to keep a smile in my voice! I actually find myself having more fun with life.

The whole family noticed the change and wondered what had happened to change my disposition. I would like to thank that young girl (wherever she may be) for giving me a new outlook on life. Grandchildren can influence how we behave.

Happy Bob, Gallatin

Dear Happy Bob,

What a lucky family to be living with you. It is too bad many of us do not take criticism or suggestions so eagerly. The fact that you want your Grandchildren to see you as a pleasant person testifies to your unselfish love.

We all need to remember that nobody wants to hear how we feel! This reminds me of the woman who knew her family had stopped listening to her afflictions. She commissioned her monument years before her death to read, "*See, I Told You I Was Sick!*"

We all need to remember that most young people rarely listen to any criticism. A long-haired multi-millionaire shared in a seminar that he had made his money in spite of a Grandfather telling him, "You won't amount to anything until you get your hair cut!"

Aristotle would want us to remember that: "Happiness is an expression of the soul in action." Exciting Grandparents, like Bob, prove to young people that love comes from within and not by the gifts we may bestow.

Q: My daughter and her husband have stated emphatically, "We don't want any children, so stop asking!"

I think they are over-reacting to the state of the world and the economy. How can I convince them to give me some Grandchildren? They are my only opportunity. They both have good jobs and could give several children a nice home to live in.

Don't you think they are being selfish?

Tired of Waiting, Jackson

Dear Tired Mother,

It really isn't important what I think; what matters are the choices your daughter and son-in-law have made with their lives. Many couples are opting not to begin a family until later, and then there are those who choose to remain childless. For whatever their reasons, you should go along with their decision. It is their life.

What do you mean by "*several* children"? If you need to hold babies or read to young children, go out and do some volunteer work. Hospitals and schools everywhere would always welcome dedicated volunteer Grandparents.

If you have additional time and would relish the idea of children and extra money, open up an after-school or a mother's day out program.

You cannot expect your children to fulfill your needs. Don't depend on them for your happiness. As our Granddaughters say, "Get a life" of your own.

So many of my friends have no Grandchildren and have decided to simply adopt the Granddogs or Grandcats as their bragging gizmo. One of my friends recently returned from her fiftieth-year reunion. She explained to an understanding group that when the Grandchildren albums started coming around, she pulled her album out and passed it along with the rest—astonished classmates endured twenty-five different poses of her cat, Kitty Creamcheese!

I can't imagine expecting your children to supply you with entertainment.

CHILDREN SPEAK OUT

Q: My Grandmother reads your column and she might get the hint if you help me out. I am fifteen years old and I love my Grandparents very much, but I don't like to go over there. I do like to go to visit my friends' Grandparents because theirs are fun. I don't mean just because they take us places or have a forty-two-inch TV, but because they talk about interesting things.

My Grandfather doesn't say much of anything, but when he does, I like to listen. He tells me about when he lived in Kentucky and the games he and his brothers played.

My Grandmother only fusses about things, complains about her health, and constantly tells me how easy my life is. I have tried to talk to her about her childhood, but she says it wasn't interesting.

Is there any way I can make them understand that I really want to be a part of their lives, but they have to help me out? How do I talk to them?

Lonely, Knoxville

Dear Lonely,

You sound like a very mature teenager. I admire you for recognizing why you don't visit often and that you actually want to change things. I hope your Grandmother is as willing as you seem to be about improving the relationship.

When you go over there, have a mental list of your activities to tell your Grandparents and talk fast. Maybe if her mind is taken off of her own problems, she will be able to concentrate on your life more.

Are you able to spend some time alone with your Grandfather? It sounds like the two of you need and enjoy each other's company. He probably doesn't get much of an opportunity to relive his happier days with someone he loves and a lot of teenagers wouldn't be as interested as you are.

Have you discussed your feelings with your own parents? They need to understand your resistance to going for visits. They probably can't change your Grandmother, but communication with them is extremely important.

Note to Granny: Wake up and realize nobody *has* to visit you. Your Granddaughter is trying very hard to do her duty by you and you are blowing the opportunity. Remember, nobody wants to listen to somebody complain. If you will start listening to those around you and start caring about their projects, you'll find your own life becoming much more interesting and you might even begin to see more visitors.

LEAVING A LEGACY

Q: I have never seen any of my Grandparents. My father's parents lived in Spain and died before I could ever meet them. My mother was adopted and never really felt that she had a family. I never knew her adoptive parents. I grew up longing for touchable Grandparents.

My Spanish Grandmother had prepared a book for me about my father's family. She had completed three generations and included pictures that were labeled and had stories to go with each one. She had written the most beautiful love story about how she had met my Grandfather and how they fell in love. She followed that with a touching story of the birth of my father. There were pictures to go along with his growing up years.

I am a college student and read one of your columns about written memories being "the greatest gift of all." Although I have never met them, I feel as if my Grandmother truly did give me the greatest gift when she left me their story.

I wanted you to know that what you said was true. Keep telling other Grandparents to do this for their Grandchildren. Even though they may be able to hold them and tell them stories, children do forget. I have friends who have read my memories and wish for the same.

Carol D., Chattanooga

Dear Carol,

Thank you for reminding all of us that an inheritance often appears in the form of the indefinable and mysterious. If all I had left to remind me of my parents and Grandparents were memories, I would possess a fortune.

They may not have known they also left me with a knowledge of love, patience, and understanding, but these were gifts that were given through their own acts of kindness, courtesy, and acceptance.

Several members of our families have done a lot of research and written several booklets about various sides of the Bensons, Swallows, Stephens, and Rich genealogy. It means so much to be able to identify yourself as being a small part of a greater family.

Q: I keep reading about the need for me to write about my life for my Grandchildren. I cannot get started! I have never liked to write, never learned to type, and also hate the idea of speaking into a tape recorder.

My daughter even bought me one of those memory books for Grandmothers. I only have to fill in the blanks, but can't even make myself do that!

Any more bright ideas?

Suzanne, Cookeville

Dear Suzanne,

If you can make a grocery list, you can jot down entries in your memory book. Shame on you!

For those of you who don't like to take pen to paper and create a story for your descendants, maybe the latest style of scrapbooks will motivate you. If you haven't attended a scrapbooking workshop, you have missed out on a lot of fun and information. Two women decided that their family pictures lacked individuality, plus they saw a need to preserve valuable photographs. Their method of scrapbooking and journaling has sparked an interest all over the United States.

To produce a family legacy, these albums can be an appropriate inspiration. How many black and white photographs (fifty or sixty years old) do you have in a box? How many are labeled as to their names, relationship, or importance? How long are they going to remain in that condition?

If necessary, do some family research and label all those individuals. Make sure you identify how they are related to you and if you know a story about them, journal beside the picture.

You might want to begin your photo scrapbook on an easier theme—maybe your high school years. Jot down a phrase or two for each picture and present this to your teenage Grandchildren. Maybe an updated baby book of your own children for their next birthday.

We complain that we do not have the time, but which is more important—those senseless TV programs or the creation of a family heirloom?

If you need some inspiration, find a workshop or store and start "cropping" pictures.

Q: In one of your columns, you talked about doing scrapbooks for your Grandchildren. I thought you might like to know about an unusual scrapbook that was made for my daughter.

She had been interested in some of our family's genealogical research for our family tree. For her birthday, my mother presented her with a scrapbook made out of a loose-leaf binder with divided sections. Each section included a mini-biography on a person in her history, a page of photographs, and in most cases a collection of writings by that person. With the exception of my brother, all of the individuals listed in the book are a direct female line. It seems that many of our people enjoyed writing.

The section on me includes several letters that I had written home from college and some from overseas when I was in the military. I traveled a lot in those days and wrote extensive travelogues home.

Then comes the section on the producer of the scrapbook—my daughter's maternal Grandmother. She wrote a lot of poetry from elementary school forward and she tried her hand at children's books when she was older. I can see many of my life experiences in her stories that she shared with my daughter.

Great-Grandmother was an elementary school teacher. One summer she took a class on children's literature. The scrapbook has copies of several stories that she wrote for class assignments.

Great-great-Grandmother had a rather unhappy marriage. She wrote a great deal of poetry and short stories to rejoice in the pleasure of her children and how she coped with the many disappointments in her life.

My daughter has used this book several times for school projects. She also looks forward to her Grandmother visiting (once a year) and going through the book together.

Joni, Oak Ridge

Dear Joni,

If this doesn't induce some Grandparents to get with the scrapbook project, nothing will! So get out the picture boxes, pencil, and paper and begin some history for your Grandchildren.

Q: I keep reading about your scrapbook suggestions and I have made this my hobby since I retired.

I have a son, a daughter, four Grandchildren, and eight great-Grandchildren. My scrapbooks are made for each individual.

I make not just picture albums (although I do use photos), but include grade cards, news items, appropriate cartoons, birthday cards, etc. So you can see these are truly scrap books.

I use loose-leaf books because something old is always showing up. I attempt to keep things in chronological order, but often times a baby picture shows up when the child is maybe six or seven years old.

When the scrapbook is full, I use it as a Christmas or birthday gift, put a check inside, and my shopping is done. My family seems to look forward to each edition.

Ruth, Nashville

Dear Ruth,

What a sensible idea—putting many things in the scrapbook. We have put too much emphasis on pure photo albums recently. I especially like the idea of adding current news clippings and cartoons. I have saved cartoons for years and now I can begin to add those to scrapbooks.

Several other concepts that I have seen lately are theme albums. Ideas for Grandchildren might be a special trip taken together, birthday parties, beginning school days, a picture book of all the animals you have had in your life, etc. Family themes could be a fortieth birthday, anniversary parties, baby or wedding showers, rehearsal dinners, or the progressive building of a new home.

For those of you who haven't visited the scrapbook section of many stores, you will find a multitude of stickers to add to the creativeness of your pages.

Don't be afraid to make a small collection. We don't have to show a lifetime or even cover several years to create an album. My step-daughter, Barbara Elizabeth, just compiled a beautiful book on the trip she and her mother took to Maine.

Saving memories is the key! Tennessee Williams said, "Life is all memory, except for the one present moment that goes by so quick you hardly catch it going."

Q: I just heard a woman say she didn't want her children to know her family history and she couldn't stand her voice on the recorder.

I couldn't believe her fears and she should hear my crackly, weak voice. But that is the sound my Granddaughter knows, and I doubt if she thinks it sounds all that bad.

I think it is a thrill to convince my Grandchildren that I did not have a television during my years of growing up. They also have trouble realizing that automobiles did not have power steering or automatic windows, or radio and CD players, or keys that lock and unlock remotely.

We lived in a farming community; there were all the chores of getting the harvest taken care of. There is nothing as much fun as sitting with a sheller and shelling popcorn and popping it right then, or making fudge or taffy. We even made our own toys.

We rolled a tire, made a tire or bag swing, dug holes in the sand and made frog houses, climbed trees, and so many more things I could tell. The days weren't long enough.

We visited our family on the Mississippi River and watched the tow boats and fishermen. We picked up pecans and hickory nuts, and had a cookout second to none.

Our hogs made the sausage we fried, our eggs came from our henhouse, our milk came from our cows, and we sat on a log near the fires and I have never tasted anything better than the foods we fixed.

I think you get the picture of why I found it so wonderful to tell my Granddaughter what I could remember about our lives before television. By the way, she lives nearly a thousand miles from me so most of this conversation was on the telephone (which we also didn't have in our home as I was growing up).

So keep preaching about how wonderful and easy it is to tell your stories to your Grandchildren.

Lois, Columbia

Dear Lois,

What a wonderful story. Too many people put off recounting history for unimportant reasons.

Another reader wrote about the book she hand-typed for her Grandchildren. She said it took her three years and she was so proud of it. What a priceless legacy!

I want my Grandchildren to know things about me that no one else will remember. For instance, the first time I went to a large wedding, I asked my mother, "When are the pallbearers coming in?" And the time I won a blue ribbon at the fair for riding my pony. The boy contestants said I won because I was a *girl*! Oh well.

BEGINNING YOUR MEMOIRS

1. Who are you compiling this information for? How many copies will you need?

2. Fill in your personal genealogy charts. You should have four sections to begin—your parents and their parents. Make a list of relatives, friends, or neighbors you want to call or write for information you need.

3. Outline subject and periods you want to cover.

4. Pull out pictures and identify with names, dates, and stories about them.

5. Plan on a visit to a large public library and ask for their section on genealogy research. They will be more than glad to help you learn how to explore the history of your family.

6. Look on the computer for many web sites designed to help you find out more information.

7. Handwritten pages are wonderful to pass on to family, but if you are producing a lot of material, have trouble with pen and paper, or do not have access to a typewriter or computer, hire someone to put the information on a computer disk.

The most important factor is for you to enjoy what you are doing. As you walk back through your past and remember the joys, the happiness, and the peaks, don't forget the importance of the sad times, the difficult changes, and the strength *you* gained from your life's walk. Remember, *you are leaving a legacy*!

Chapter 2

STEPINLAWS

A New Blend of Families

AS WE ARE PLUNGED INTO THE ROLE OF GRANDPARENT, there comes along a multitude of in-laws. I have never met anyone who hasn't dealt with some new adjustments to this role. Most people find it immensely frustrating. In-laws may come from a different culture, various backgrounds, other states, other environments— some even seem to come from other planets. But no matter whom they are or what they may be, our children have chosen to be a part of that family; if we want to be a part of the scene, we have to inter- mingle and behave!

The old saying, "You can choose your friends, but not your family" goes along with your children's choices.

There are many topics we need to think about. Are we going to be understanding of all the changes that will come?

* How do we make sure the in-laws don't become out-laws?

* Are we going to be an overbearing in-law or will we adapt to others ideas?

* What are we going to call each other? (This should be a discus- sion to be confronted early in the game to prevent awkwardness to either side. Many daughters-in-law never call their mother- in-law anything until a child comes along and "Granny" finally gets a name!)

The men deal with: "Who do I call Mom? What should I say you are? Mother-in-law still sounds like a wicked witch."

Many of us have been involved with the in-law reality for a long time and let me remind you, we are never too old to learn a new way to do something. We are never so wise that we can't take advice from someone younger or different.

We all need to learn to balance our loyalties and keep in mind that a husband and wife make up a unit—*not* mother, daughter, and son-in-law!

How do we make sure the people we love can all get along? Or at least not end up hating each other? How do we handle those in-laws who just don't like us, even if we are the "perfect" relative?

Now that we have said all this, be reminded that Grandchildren come along and changes begin all over again. How can we be sure that we show maturity and change with the tide as new names, new advice (or not), new rules, and new attitudes come into play?

My mother always reminded me that, "You marry the whole family when you pick a husband." We all know this to be very true. We have to make allowances and be grown up, even when we might rather pitch a fit.

Remember: Be humble and loving.

Q: *You once wrote that the way to avoid some of the Grandparenting problems that come with the divorce of a son and daughter-in-law is to keep a good relationship along the way. I have tried to be good to my daughter-in-law, but she is rather standoffish and I haven't been able to build much of a compatibility with her. I don't suspect any problems with them as a couple, but your words made me aware of the fact that she and I really don't have much in common.*

Can you give me some advice on how to break through the wall of communication?

Charlotte, Carthage

Dear Charlotte,

My first words of advice came to me through a newlywed talking about her new mother-in-law. The young bride was complaining that, "she always treats him so special and acts like she simply tolerates me."

Rule #1: When your child marries, they become as one. Do not make a difference in how you treat them individually. If you are going to, make sure you are leaning more to the newest member of the family.

At this point for you, I might suggest you take her to lunch or some special event, just the two of you. It will give you an opportunity to bond outside the togetherness of the couple.

Rule #2: Keep your opinions to yourself. Let them make their own decisions, right or wrong, they will learn together. Don't even try to be subtle—they will read through your attempts every time.

You might call her occasionally for advice on some concerns you may be facing. Maybe take her shopping to help you buy a needed piece of furniture or clothing.

Rule #3: Make sure your new family member becomes an integral part of the spouse's clan by creating a calendar of family birthdays and important anniversaries including important dates in her family. What they choose to do with the information is up to them, but being aware will help them to experience a sense of belonging.

Don't go overboard pushing your attention. Take it slow and build a relationship that is genuine and honest.

Q: *When my daughter married, I had read all the books on how to be a good mother-in-law and felt like I was well prepared. I promised to keep my mouth zipped and never give advice without being "pressured."*

I made it through the wedding with my son-in-law apparently still thinking I was "almost perfect." I didn't call on their honeymoon. I didn't unpack their boxes in their apartment while they were gone. They were back eight days and two hours before I called to invite them over to eat.

They have been married for six months. I have not offered to do their laundry, take them home-cooked meals, or insist her new husband help with the housework.

My problem is his mother! She has done all those things. I didn't even get a chance to be in the way. She has also announced her Thanksgiving plans and is already planning on their appearance Christmas morning.

I thought about talking to my daughter, but she apparently is enjoying all the attention. The new mother-in-law has scooped my daughter under her wing as if she didn't have a mother. She has taken her to lunch at her club, taken her shopping, and even hired someone to make new curtains for their apartment—and she picked out the fabric!

As a mother-in-law, what should I do without looking like the notorious nagging "other woman"?

Carol, Smyrna

Dear Carol,

She sounds as if she already has a voodoo doll made up of you and will stick pins in it as soon as you make the wrong move.

There will always be the one who decides Thanksgiving and Christmas dates. For some of us, there are even stepparents who have a say in the selection pool for holidays. I try to play Saint Barbara and wait until all schedules are made and then pick what works for me.

Most of us just sit and wait for the new to wear off and the waters to calm. Maybe your daughter is also trying to be the perfect daughter-in-law. If she continues to leave you out, I would tell her how proud you are of her new status, but remind her you miss those mother/daughter days.

READERS RESPOND TO READERS

The previous column on mothers-in-law responded to the question of how to deal with the "other" mother-in-law.

In that column, I made the statement that I try to be "Saint Barbara" when it comes to scheduling holidays. I have always been willing to let the others make the choices and I, sweetly and humbly, take what is left.

My precious, darling sons wanted me to consider sharing some of my "not so saintly" acts as a mother-in-law. I couldn't imagine what on earth they were talking about, but their list came quickly and categorically.

Since some of you may be under the assumption that I have always done everything by the book, made no mistakes, and have a clear vision of what is expected of me in every relationship, I am simply going to say, "That would be incorrect."

I guess I could tell you about the weekend that I decided to cut my Granddaughter Jessica's hair. I knew they would be so thrilled that I had saved them money and be very impressed that my ever sharp cross-stitch scissors helped me to create a new hairstyle. They were not thrilled or impressed. They should have told me they were trying to let her hair grow!

Then there was the time I put our six-month-old Grandson, Sean, on a quilt beside our bed to sleep for the night. I was afraid that I wouldn't hear him in his bed down the hall, and I know he loved it when I held his tiny hand as he went to sleep. I guess I should have remembered how babies slip and slide around all night. He woke me up the next morning crying, from under the middle of our bed, stuck between the legs and a blanket box. It did take us moving the mattress off the bed to get him out and we didn't do it again, but they still like to remind me of the slip of judgment.

I won't tell you about the watermelon and cotton candy episode or the surprise with the tape recorder, but I will say, "I am doing better." They even agreed that as I get older I seem to make fewer blunders that create family misapprehension.

Q: I am the mother of two children. My husband's mother—their Grandmother—is driving me crazy. What do you do when your mother-in-law lives in the same house with you? She acts like she is the head of our household. I can't get my husband to straighten this situation out.

She insists on doing all the shopping—food, clothes, household items, etc. Last week she called a painter and had all of our rooms repainted while we were at work. We own the house!

How do you suggest I make him be a man and stop allowing her to be so domineering?

Theida, Jamestown

Dear Theida,

The record-breaking heat and humidity must be getting to every form of life. An outbreak of dramatic dog and snake bites has reached uncommon numbers, and in the last month I have received several mother-in-law complaints similar to the one above. All of them were colorfully detailed accusations of mistreatment. Christine from Old Hickory said her mother-in-law was trying to "transform my husband into a Mama's Boy!" Marlene from Nashville said, "My mother-in-law calls ten times a day to see if I am appropriately dealing with her social clubs!" Columbia, Tennessee's mother-in-law would probably win the prize for Grandchild discrimination!

Since I was fortunate to have had an "almost perfect" mother-in-law (we disagreed over our political affiliations), I took these problems to my Real Life group. Marjorie said, "They all live too close! Move out of the house! If possible, move out of town."

The group gave a second unanimous ruling: "Never try to place your husband in the middle." (They said "husband" because all agree that 90 percent of in-law trouble is directed toward the mother of the son.) You are then asking him to choose between wife and mother. This should never be an alternative. A man needs his best friend and lover to be his spouse. He will always desire an understanding and devoted mother—one who has forgotten his dirty, stinky socks and repulsive habits.

Real Life is a group of senior adults who have seen it all. They have had mothers-in-law, and they all now possess the title. "Mothers-in-law are too often stereotyped as critical and demanding," declared Helen.

Most of the group dearly loved their mothers-in-law and felt they had a good relationship with their own daughters-in-law. "Try to see mothers-in-law as human beings with emotional pains—the same as you suffer. She may need you as a friend, but if this is impossible—be civil," maintained Annette.

Learn from our experience!

Q: My daughter-in-law is very sweet, very good to our Grandchildren, and an excellent mother, but she never hugs or shows any physical affection for them. I want to say something to her, but my son says, "No." He says she can't help it because her entire family is that way. Is there anything I can do?

Loving Person, Sweetwater

Dear Loving Person,

I have heard this story many times through our Grandparenting group. Somewhere along the way, some of us failed to teach "directed affection" to our children. It always hurts to see a child that has never been held or snuggled. In one of Bob Hope's more serious moments he said, "Children that aren't cuddled—curdle."

Your daughter-in-law may have learned from parents that felt too little was better than too much, but there is a difference in "smothering love" and the "just-right" kind. All of us need to touch and be touched. It is an immediate and a warm way of saying, "I care about you." Our need to be touched, caressed, and cuddled is as basic as our need for food.

Does your daughter-in-law recoil when you put your arms around her? She may want it as much as anyone, but is afraid. Ask her if she minds you hugging your Grandchildren. I cannot imagine her refusing your request. Then, hug them all you want to!

Our group suggests you make sure your son is giving them an extra portion of cuddling. If she continues to be distant with everyone you might "gently" suggest to your son that counseling might be good for her!

Q: *This is a problem with my mother-in-law, who happens to be the Grandmother of my two sons. I have tried to teach them responsibility and every time we plan a family event, she is always late. Not just a few minutes, but an hour or two. I think this comes under personal responsibility. How do I explain this to my sons? They have asked why she does this and why they can't say anything to her.*

Sue, Columbia

Dear Sue,

My "face up to reality" husband would tell you to tell her son to say something to her. He should suggest to her that your sons do not understand why she is always late. Ask her to explain to them each time she is tardy. She shouldn't get by with, "I just lost track of time," or "someone called as I was walking out," or "traffic was bad." Those things should only happen one time!

His way is correct, but I have a difficult time confronting people. I would tell your sons that being on time is an individual responsibility. In my book, people who are late are self absorbed. They think everything should revolve around their lifestyle. People who are constantly changing plans, after the occasion is scheduled, also show a lack of concern for other people's arrangement. John F. Kennedy was speaking at Vanderbilt University in May of 1963, and he stated, "Our privileges can be no greater than our obligations. The protection of our rights can endure no longer than the performance of our responsibilities." In other words, we can't have the good stuff if we are not reliable with our obligations and commitments.

We have moved beyond the "me" generation and those folks need to grow up. Accepting responsibility for behavior is a sign of maturity and strong character. Teach your sons that philosophy and they will go far in this great world of ours.

F. Scott Fitzgerald was quoted as saying, "Growing up is a terribly hard thing to do. It was much easier to skip and go from one childhood to another." Our world has too many of those adult children already. Thank you for teaching your sons *responsibility*!

Q: *My son recently remarried and his new bride has two children by her first marriage. How do I introduce these little girls to my friends?*

Alice, Byrdstown

Dear Alice,

How do you feel about them? What do you want them to be to you? They are now legally and officially your stepGrandchildren, but how you feel about them will dictate those introductions.

If you are welcoming them with open arms, you might say, "I want you to meet my Grand new Granddaughters, Kim and Kayla." If you are hesitant and wary of these little people in your life, you might simply say, "Kim and Kayla are my son's stepchildren."

On a personal note, one of my "stepGrandchildren" was visiting me early in our relationship, and we had gone to the pool. I noticed him talking to a new friend and asked what they had been talking about. "He asked who I was with and I told him my . . . (softly) Grandmother. Is that all right?"

"Why certainly, I tell everyone you are my Grandson." His eyes lit up as he breathed a sigh of relief and we have been best buddies ever since.

I have a biological grandchild now, but my heart can't tell the difference.

Q: *My Granddaughter is dating a young man of a different race. I am totally against this, although my son doesn't seem to care. What am I going to do or say?*
M. P., Crossville

Dear M. P.,

You are certainly allowed to express your opinion in this matter, but hopefully you will do it with a voice full of love and caring and end your summation with, "But whatever you decide, I will still be your Grandmother and love you for always."

Times are changing and your son is of a more accepting generation. We might as well face the inevitable, for if our country is to be the "melting pot of the world," all colors and nationalities will blend beautifully as they simmer into a new color. You do not have to like it, but as a caring Grandparent, you will need to accept whomever your Granddaughter chooses. Love overlooks race, religion, or social status.

Q: *I know you have talked about stepGrandchildren before, but since I didn't have any, I didn't retain much information. My daughter, who has a five-year-old daughter by a first marriage, just announced that she is getting married to a man with two teenage girls. I think I can deal with this, but is there any way we can prepare and help the transition? I have met the girls and they seem very nice, but I have heard all the stories about the wicked stepmother and I don't want my daughter to go through this.*
Betsy, Clarksville

Dear Betsy,

Statistics are telling us that 50 percent of the children in the United States are being raised in blended families. There are lots of people out there who have been there, done that, and are now prepared to tell you what works.

Every book or experienced stepparent reminds us to "prepare" and plan for what life is going to be about. The new parents need to talk—*before* the marriage—about who, what, when, where, and how they are going to deal with the situations that come up. They need to agree on acceptable behavior, including what happens when the rules are broken. They must vow to stick together and support each other through the trials of rearing any children—yours, mine, or ours.

After all this agreement, they should sit down with the children and explain the strategy. At this point, the children need to feel as if they are a part of the directional shaping and have some input on what is about to happen. After all, they probably had very little decision toward this change. The entire family needs to see itself as blended—not individuals fighting a separate process. A family is made up of unique people working together.

Don't forget, there will be ups and downs, as with a biological family, but everyone should take their time before giving up on the plan. Most professionals tell us that it takes at least three years to bond a blended family.

Now, give this column to your daughter, ask to be a part of the program, and pray that everyone is willing and cooperative.

Q: *My son is not talking to us because he says we don't treat his children equally. He says we should treat all of our Grandchildren alike. Two of them aren't our Granddaughters! They are our daughter-in-law's children. She had them when they married and now she and my son have a two-year-old boy. He is our Grandson. We don't feel we should have to buy presents for the other children. They are somebody else's Grandchildren. How can I convince my son of this?*

K. W., Nashville

Dear K. W.,

I can surely see why your son isn't talking to you. Where have you been for the last few decades? Life is changing and you have to change with it.

If your son marries a woman with two children, they are automatically your stepGrandchildren. How you treat them is up to you, but if you want any kind of a relationship with your son, I suggest you accept these new treasures into your life.

He married your daughter-in-law knowing that he was going to rear these two children, and he accepted them as his own. If you truly love your son, you will dedicate yourself to learning to love these children as he does.

Nobody can make you love them as much as you might love your own flesh and blood, but your stepGrandchildren don't need to be able to see or feel the difference. These are just *children*—not the enemy. How do you want that other set of parents to treat your Grandson? Is there some jealousy on your part? Think about all this. You sound bitter about more than just this one issue.

Q: *My six-year-old Granddaughter has a new stepfather. I am not particularly unhappy over this situation, but I don't know how to handle the matter of her biological father. She talks about him a lot, but is apparently satisfied at home with her mother and new "Dad." I am lost on how I am supposed to act or feel toward her father. Help!*

Nana, Brentwood

Dear Nana,

You are going through the stages a majority of Grandparents are facing today. A first-grade teacher-friend related that she had thirty students and twenty-eight of them had two sets of parents. We are going to need a book of etiquette on this soon!

Pearl, a dear friend, said her ex-son-in-law's picture continues to hang on her wall because, "He is still Autumn's father, although she calls her stepfather 'Dad.'"

Hazel, from my Real Life group described the first time her Granddaughter asked her to help pick out a Christmas card for her father and stepmom. "It was rough, but Jennie wouldn't have understood my not wanting to. So I did!"

The consensus of opinion seems to be that you remain on a reasonable relationship with ex-in-laws in order to make the transition uncomplicated for Grandchildren. It may not always be easy, but remember, children will invariably love their biological parent, no matter what they have done! You should respect those feelings.

Q: *I want to tell you about our extended family. I married a man who has three daughters and a stepson. I have three daughters. One of them married a man who had two children. This way, I inherited three Grandchildren from the stepson, one from one of my husband's daughters and two stepchildren from my daughter. I have had them all here at one time. We live on the lake, so it's a lot like "camping out." Now we are on a new set of Grandkids from my girls—ages four, six, and ten.*

My Nashville daughters call all these folks we accumulate through marriage and divorce "stepinlaws"—all in one word. This saves a lot of explaining.

Karen, Cookeville

Dear Karen,

I love it! "Stepinlaws"!! Webster will surely pick up on this new word soon. Also, thanks to Charlene R. Sisco of Madison, who shared her love for her family of "steps" with me. We are all enjoying the blend!

One of our Granddaughters asked, "Wow, which one of you is the step? I can't tell the difference." Hopefully, all families are filled with goodwill and determination to share their family life without "telling the difference."

There are people who want to talk about "blood kin" and "married kin." As long as there is a love that bonds through all the twine, nothing else matters. Love is shown by affection, sensitivity, and not by making a distinction between "blood" and "the other kind." Don't forget Herbert Hoover's counsel that, "Children are our most valuable natural resource!"

Many Grandparents talk to me of working at not communicating discrimination among their blended families. It must be a real concern with numerous people.

A touch of amusement from one of ours: He asked his mother how old I was. After she told him, he replied, "Well, she is pretty to be so old."

Q: You asked for letters about families with "steps." I am so proud of how our family has developed. We love all of our Grandchildren equally! Our daughter had two daughters and married a man with two sons. All six of them went to a minister who worked with blended families before they married. He gave them three rules and they have continued to abide by them for ten years!

THE RULES WERE:

1. Mother and Daddy must stick together with discipline. If you don't stand together, you won't make it.

2. Never force kids to love each other. They do have to treat each other as well as they treat their neighbors.

3. Kids must work out problems among themselves. Parents don't solve their fights.

Amy, Franklin

Dear Amy,

Congratulations to your family! These rules would fit any family or any relationship. We should all be trying harder to stick together, treat everyone fairly, and solve all difficulties with the person involved.

I realize there are days I am too simplistic in my attitude about life, but Robert Fulghum's advice in *All I Really Need to Know I*

Learned in Kindergarten would settle almost every predicament we have to deal with. "Share everything. Play fair. Don't hit people. Put things back where you found them. Clean up your own mess. Don't take things that aren't yours. Say you're sorry when you hurt somebody. Wash your hands before you eat. Flush. Warm cookies and cold milk are good for you. Live a balanced life."

Surely to goodness, we can do that!

Q: I have two children from a first marriage and am now pregnant by my second husband. We have gotten along great with his mother for the first two years. She seemed to welcome my children into her life as if they were her own. Now that I am pregnant with her son's child, she has become a changed woman.

She is acting as if there has never been another child born. This will be her first biological Grandchild. She has taken me shopping for nursery furniture (paying all the bills) and has bought enough baby clothes for six children. The problem: she now treats my children as if they are not there. She barely speaks to them. Before she would pick them up occasionally and take them places, buy them books, and even agreed to go to school on Grandparents Day.

What do I say to her? Should I have my husband talk to her?

Destiny, Knoxville

Dear Destiny,

Let's pretend we are your mother-in-law. She is about to become a "real" Grandmother in her eyes. You and your children see her as "real" and maybe she felt that way until she realized her DNA would be flowing through this child. Let's give her a chance to adjust to the momentous occasion.

Tell your children that she is caught up in the birth of this child and ask them to help her. Suggest that they take her shopping for a special gift that they can give to their new brother/sister.

StepGrandparents can be great people. They bring much to a marriage, a family, and little children. She may take a little while to put all of them in the same circle, but I am willing to wager she will come through for you. Tell her how much you appreciate how good she has been to your children and that you recognize what a wonderful Grandparent she has already become.

Make sure your husband understands the drama that is going on. He is also going to become a different role player in your equation. If he can grasp the possible pitfalls, he might just prevent any problems at all.

Now, what will they *all* call the Grandmother?

Q: *When I married my husband, I had a two-year-old daughter by a previous marriage. His family has always been good to her, but now that we have a daughter of our own, his Grandmother pays absolutely no attention to my five-year-old. She originally gave her more attention than anyone and would often refer to her as her "first Grandchild." Now, she comes over and offers to feed and baby-sit for the baby and completely ignores the pleas of our other daughter. She has even asked me, "Why doesn't Mama like me anymore?"*

My parents live a great distance from us and never see either child. His Grandmother will never have other Grandchildren. I haven't said anything to my husband. I don't want him to think I am being selfish or petty. What can I say to my daughter?

Debbie, Chattanooga

Dear Debbie,

Growing up I often heard the expression, "blood is thicker than water," referring to how blood relations are given more care and concern than non-blood relatives. I never understood because it sounded like if you weren't blood related, you were unimportant. Some people still react this way. Your Grandmother-in-law may have enjoyed the thrill of your daughter until she got a "blood Grandchild." I hope this is not true with her. Maybe she just needs time to adjust to a baby. After all, she missed that stage with your first child.

Try to explain this to your daughter in front of Mama and tell her they will both need to do some "grown-up" activities together soon. Tell Mama how much she has meant to your first child and that you hope she will continue to be a vital part of both of your children's lives.

Family relationships take time and patience. I can almost guarantee that in a few months or a few years, Mama will not make a difference between the girls—if *you* don't create a difference!

You do need to talk to your husband about your concerns before there is more of a problem than this. Blended families are difficult enough without spouses harboring secret feelings.

Q: I jumped into a marriage that included a teenage stepson, and I am not having a good time! I thought I could get along, but he is about to wear out my last string of sanity. I am shocked that I am having such intense feelings of dislike for this child. He is obnoxious, disagreeable, lazy, and very unloving! I don't want to be around him and yet my husband has given me the task of raising this child! I love my husband, but am afraid this is going to break up our marriage.

Melissa, (e-mail)

Dear Melissa,

First of all, you are not alone in your dilemma. There are other mothers who feel the same way, and the children were born from their own bodies. Many teenagers can be a pain at times.

I have often said that one night my youngest son went to bed as a loving, sweet twelve-year-old and woke up the next morning a thirteen-year-old alien who had nothing in common with his immediate family. He dressed funny, exhibited bad manners, and refused to talk in his old language. This foreigner lived with us for several years and miraculously one day the "real" son came back home.

The famed authority on child-rearing, Charles Dobson, was quoted as saying, "Teenagers should be placed in a barrel, fed regularly, and then released at a more appropriate time." He would go on to tell you that time, prayer, and patience (outside the barrel) will get you through that troubling year. You do need to sit down with your husband and make sure the two of you are sharing this experience. He needs to be the authority figure and give you some relief from the complications of being the "stepmom." If this continues, I would suggest counseling before the marriage becomes the first tragedy of this experience. Teenagers are supposed to undergo a slow process of learning, but a marriage must continually grow, day-by-day.

Q: My stepGranddaughter is getting married this summer and she has invited us to the wedding. My husband's ex-wife will be there, and she has made it extremely clear that she doesn't want me there. I would be willing to stay home, but my husband says he will not go without me.

What should I do?

Deanna, Nashville

Dear Deanna,

The etiquette of steprelationships would say to abide by the wishes of your Granddaughter and her parents. Have you discussed this with them? What do they want you to do?

The realist in me wants to know if your husband's ex-wife would care enough to make a scene. Have you had any previous dealings with her? Mannerly demeanor is required on everyone's behalf. Don't wait until one of these occasions happens. Settle the performance beforehand.

Divorce happens in the very best families, but often the children and Grandchildren are the ones to pay the price. The voice of experience to everyone involved says, "Get over it and get on with your existence." Whatever has happened is over—right or wrong, good or bad—but life does continue and no more pain should be inflicted on the innocent!

I hope you go to the wedding and everyone behaves in a "peachy-perfect" way!

Q: My ex-daughter-in-law has been so upset with my son that she refuses to let me see my Grandchildren. How do I get through to her that I'm not at fault, yet I am the one suffering the loss?

Ann, Knoxville

Dear Ann,

Divorce brings trials to all members of a family, but the children usually suffer the most confusion. Emotions are deep, hostilities are running amok, and it may fall on you, the Grandparent, to remain objective.

You will have to forget who did what and where the greatest fault should be placed. Your job is to keep foremost in your mind the emotional health of your Grandchildren. Put all this aside and plunge right into the middle of a "Grandparent maintenance program." Make the first, second, and fortieth attempt to be friends with your ex-daughter-in-law.

She wants to include you in the blame, but will eventually wear down because she does need you. Call and encourage her to talk calmly to you. Write friendly, pleasant notes to her and the Grandchildren.

Don't push the visiting part until you feel she is truly ready for this meeting. Make it a combined visit—mother *and* children—to somewhere neutral and relaxed, a fast-food restaurant, a picnic in the park, or an ice-cream parlor. You have to win the friendship of their mother, remembering you will have to maintain this attitude for a lot of years, but it is a small price to pay to have a relationship with your Grandchildren. Good luck!

Q: My Grandson drives an eighteen-wheeler and his new wife travels with him. They come through Knoxville every two months, and we are having a difficult time getting to know her. She refuses to get out of the truck.

Evelyn, Knoxville

Dear Evelyn,

Take your enthusiasm, a slice of cake, and go to her. She is probably scared, nervous, or just shy. You have no idea what pictures she has conjured up of you. Take family photographs to her, describe your household, and reminisce about your Grandson's younger days.

Who says the family parlor can't be in the front seat of a truck? Maybe she is an experienced driver and can explain all those gears to you. Meet her on her own territory. She will eventually feel comfortable enough with you.

Grandparenting is not the simple procedure it was forty years ago. Today, we are living in a new generation and have to face the facts that we must accept their lifestyles.

Q: *I am so mad at my daughter-in-law, I want to take my Grandchildren and run away. She never cooks them anything to eat. They eat at fast-food restaurants almost every night. When they come to my house, I try to feed them balanced meals and they don't even know how to eat proper food!*

She spends all her time shopping and driving them to school sports. I have talked until I am drained. My son won't take my side and I worry about what is going to happen to these children. What would you say to her?

Donna, Tullahoma

Dear Donna,

I suggest you make peace with your daughter-in-law or she may be the one running away and "taking" your Grandchildren. Listening to an attorney answer questions about Grandparent's rights, I was surprised to hear her respond: "For those of you who are trying to obtain visitation rights for your Grandchildren, I suggest you save your money. You probably are not going to win a case against the mother. For those of you who are not experiencing this crisis, prepare the way by investing in your daughter-in-law. She is the one who might later determine any visitation rights."

A nicely-dressed lady in the audience remarked, "My daughter-in-law came to me after their divorce was filed and asked, 'Are you going to be able to stay neutral? I want you to continue to see your Grandchildren.' I wanted to tell her all the angry thoughts I was harboring against her, but felt that to keep my Grandchildren I would have to zip my lip!"

Learn to accept your daughter-in-law for her good points. She must have them or your son wouldn't continue to support her. Anger often makes us blind and rarely ever gains favor with anyone!

Q: Our son and his first wife divorced when our Grandson was one year old. Both remarried. Our ex-daughter-in-law had another child by her present husband. Our son has another little boy by his present wife.

The ex-daughter-in-law was somewhat bitter and informed me I was not her new child's Grandparent. I said, "Fine, you teach your one-year-old to call me 'Mrs. Lewis.'" He would hear the "real" Grandchild call us "Nannie" and "Papa," so that's what he called us. She finally realized what a mess she was making and now we have three "Grandchildren."

I go to all three birthday parties. I buy for both families at Christmas. I buy for each member of each family on birthdays. It's so much easier to feel good about a bad situation when we all are happy. My ex-daughter-in-law will always be my Grandson's mother and her new child will always be his half-brother. There's no changing things, so make the best of a bad situation. My Grandson, Randy, would not understand why I didn't buy for his mommy and his little brother and his step dad. He loves them and thinks I should too. So do I!

(This letter was lost in the mail from July to January. When I wrote to tell her this and asked if she still wanted the letter to be printed, she replied with the following postscript.)

Since I wrote the letter to you, my son and his wife have another boy (born December 28, 1992), which makes us Grandparents to four boys. We continue to get along, and the ex-daughter-in-law sent the current daughter-in-law flowers from Randy when his new baby brother was born.

It does make split families so much closer and easier on all concerned. I would not call our family "dysfunctional" as the TV often does. I think we are very functional in more ways than one.

Alberta, Nashville,

Dear Alberta,

I think you are extremely functional and a very special Grandparent and mother-in-law.

Q: My daughter is getting a divorce and I am worried sick about what it will do to our Grandchildren. I want them to grow up in a normal family atmosphere. How can I convince my daughter that it is going to ruin their little lives?

Christine, Manchester

Dear Christine,

I suppose by "normal" family, you mean one consisting of two parents who are married to each other and only have their mutual children.

That is an ideal situation, but the majority of today's young people have more than two parents. It is not your judgment that will decide whether your daughter should get a divorce or not. She is the one living in the situation and the one to make that decision.

It will be a difficult enough conclusion without you adding to her emotional trauma. She is well aware of her mothering responsibility, and she knows the extra burden it will place on her being a single parent. Lots of children, however, survive divorce.

Your question should be: What can I be doing to lessen the disturbance in their young lives?

Spend more time with them. Try to keep their life structured as before. Talk about what has happened and listen to their fears. Remain positive, reassuring them everything will be all right. Work especially hard on holidays and birthdays.

You cannot solve the problem, but you can soothe the circumstance.

Q: My husband and I are devastated. Our only son just informed us he is getting a divorce and his wife will be getting custody of our two Grandchildren. He will have very liberal visitations, but we are so mad! We certainly see why our son is so anxious to divorce this two-faced woman, but they are definitely putting us in a very insecure and despicable position. What do most Grandparents do when this happens?

Justine, Livingston

Dear Justine,

Your lengthy letter demonstrates a barrel full of antagonism. Hopefully you will be able to bridle this verbal hostility for the sake of your Grandchildren. Change your focus to:

1. The children are probably more hurt and confused than you are!

2. Your daughter-in-law has the upper hand in determining the relationship and visitation you will have with your Grandchildren.

3. Put your feelings aside. Do not take sides. Listen to your Grandchildren when they are with you. Allow them to blow off steam and support their fragile emotions. This may not always be easy on you when the time comes for them to lash out at your "beloved son" or defend their mother. *Just* listen!

Remind them your neutral house will always be a haven of love and joy. Endeavor to make your visits a fun time and a pleasant break from the tension going on with their distracted parents. Plan occasions that will offer some semblance of a normal life.

Discipline yourselves to maintain a working relationship with your ex-daughter-in-law. She can make or break the connection you have with your Grandchildren. Remind her that you will not takes sides in front of the children and that you will continue to be working together as Grandparents which she has every right to expect.

This choice was not made with you or the Grandchildren in mind. You all are like the little goldfish plucked out of the familiar tank at the pet store. You are never sure where you are going or what variety of different containers you will end up in next, but keep swimming and never attack the mother sharks!

Q: *We have a beautiful six-year-old Granddaughter from our only son. She lives with her mom, who is living at home with her parents, sister, brother-in-law, and their baby. Our son has stayed very involved with his daughter. They love each other very much.*

We and our son don't feel like our Granddaughter is being taken care of. We have tried many times to talk to them about it, but they always have an excuse. Most of the time they say our Granddaughter didn't want to do the things we see as needing improvements—such as a bath every night, brushing her teeth every day, and wearing clothes that are too small. She is in the first grade and we don't want her to go to school looking this way. We buy her clothes, but they don't let her wear them. They say she doesn't like them.

We have talked to our Granddaughter many times about the importance of taking baths and brushing her teeth and hair. She does great at our house, but goes back to what she can get away with as soon as she gets home.

Any suggestions from your group?

Concerned, Hartsville

Dear Concerned,

The Real Life group said you are fighting a losing battle. When the Grandchild is living with Mom, Grandparents, aunts, uncles, and cousins—and they live with a different standard of cleanliness and dress—you are not going to be able to change anything at this point.

Hazel Whitehead suggested that you remember most six-year-olds never want to take a bath. Hazel Jones said that she can remember dressing her six-year-old son in clean matching clothes and sending him off to school, only to find out later that he was taking play clothes and changing on the way.

Ural Campbell, a widow who won a National Parenting Award for successfully rearing three children alone in such an exemplary manner, wanted you to think about the more important issues for a child—encouragement, good moral advice, and a pleasant visit for her to remember.

Relax. Someday when she is living in the bathroom and spending too much money on clothes, you will laugh at this concern!

Q: Our next-door neighbor's Grandson was kidnapped by his non-custodial father. We have been so upset. A counselor came and talked to all of us neighbors about how we can be more alert to what is going on in all families. She gave us a pamphlet that says 350,000 kids are taken from their homes by non-custodial parents every year. The paper also gave us some tips to teach our Grandchildren:

1. *Practice dialing "911" with your Grandchildren. By age three they should know your address, area code, and phone number.*

2. *Tell them constantly you will always love them, would never agree to their parent or a stranger taking them, and you will always keep looking for them if they disappear.*

3. *Role-play identifying safe strangers such as fast-food servers, gas attendants, police officers, grocery clerks, or teachers at new schools and asking them for help.*

4. *Pick a code word known only to you and your Grandchild. Advise them never to go with someone unless they are given the password.*

She also talked to us about watching non-custodial parents. If they quit their job, disconnect the phone, or sell their home—better watch out!

I hope this will help other Grandparents not have to go through what our neighbor has experienced.

Anonymous

Dear Concerned Neighbor,

Thank you for the information. We all assume this will not happen to us, but the possibility may be just around the corner. I think teaching this same information would apply to any stranger picking up children. We don't want to frighten them needlessly, but they do need some skills for combating the sick individuals that abound in our world. As we continue to see the security and safety of our schools slip away, I am reminded of Anne Lindbergh's statement, "Only in growth, reform and change is true security to be found"

We are the generation that grew up leaving doors unlocked and having no fear for our own safety. We may be the generation that is going to have to get busy and unravel the causes of these tribulations.

Chapter 3

OVER THE RIVER AND THROUGH THE WOODS

Long-Distance, Travel, and Holidays

WHEN I WAS A CHILD, MY MATERNAL GRANDPARENTS lived a few miles away and my paternal Grandmother lived in the next county (before she moved in with us). Today, children are put on planes to fly across several states to visit their Grandparents. Some may not know their Grandparents until they are of school-age or older.

Going on a vacation with my Grandparents was never an option. They didn't take vacations! Spending days at their house was not seen as a vacation, but a visit.

Today, it is very common to load up the Grandchildren and take off for exciting venues.

What an astonishing new world we all enjoy. It is thrilling to watch the Baby Boomers adapting their eventful lives to draw in a circle of Grandchildren—to watch as they anticipate a new and rewarding connection with their children and plan for future activities.

Yes, they may be traveling in a super-deluxe van or all-equipped motor home, with the electronic entertainment being channeled into tiny ears and eyes. They wear matching T-shirts and proclaim a fresh tradition has begun! This is our world!

How we maintain the long-distance Grandparenting is extensive and unlimited—thanks to our latest technology.

How we deal with those holidays, which are becoming more numerous, is still as dramatic as ever. Some families just cannot break away from tradition!

Q: I have five Grandchildren and they have all been able to visit us this summer. We don't want to let this closeness slip by as they travel back home. They all live more than five hundred miles away from us, and we may not see some of them until next summer. How can we maintain this relationship?

Mary, Crossville

Dear Mary,

You are one of the millions of long-distance Grandparents. This is another of the phenomena of this new generation. When you and I were growing up, Granny lived "over the river and through the woods."

Mimi Agnes found out early it took a lot of imagination to communicate long-distance. One of her favorite methods was to become an animal and write pen-pal letters to her small Grandchildren from the pet. Pinky the Rabbit, Sammie the Squirrel, and Eleanor the Elephant spend a lot of time telling the Grandchildren about their way of life and what was going on back home at Mimi's house.

G. G. Marion keeps a diary of the various things that she does in a week. She is a volunteer in a nursing home, and her diary is filled with interesting stories of the people who live there. When little Mark comes to visit, she has an abundance of fascinating stories to read to him; Mark is developing a sense of concern for others.

Papa Glenn is a gardener, and he began sending his Granddaughter a special packet of seeds each spring. The packet contained a few of everything Glenn had planted and soon little Kayla was shouting, "My tomatoes have blooms! Call Papa!"

When Norma cleaned out her upstairs closet, she found lots of pictures of her son when he was a young boy. She selected the best five, pasted them in a small book, mailed the book to her Grandson and explained: "I will mail more pictures later. You can keep this a secret between us and we will surprise your dad someday."

As Nana Judy found articles in her weekly newspaper that she thought her older Grandchildren would enjoy, she would clip them and attach them to sheets of paper with her own thoughts and opinions.

There are numerous other ways to stay involved. Subscribe to the same magazine for you and the Grandchildren or start a story book together.

Now, wipe away those lonesome tears and select one of the suggestions. You can narrow the distance and maintain the relationship with those waiting Grandchildren.

Q: *We have two Grandchildren here in Knoxville, three in Florida, two in Colorado, and one in Louisiana. It is very simple to show the ones in Knoxville we care, but how do we show the others? They get presents on birthdays and Christmas, but only see us once every year or two. We don't have much money to spend, so lots of gifts are out.*

Emily, Knoxville

Dear Emily,

The fact you are concerned about showing them love is the first step. Many adults have a difficult time demonstrating the positive manner of concern for their Grandchildren.

For some people "love" means approval. Love should be unconditional for the sweet, cute youngsters as well as the long-haired, hippy teenager. We don't have to approve of someone to love them. We don't even have to like their ways. Love says, "I care about you, no matter what!"

Young people will probably not be as good at communicating by mail as you, but after all you were asking how to show them *you* care. Send them your favorite cartoons. Find articles about subjects that interest you. Grampa Kenny keeps all varieties of clippings to send to his sports enthusiasts. He even borrows the neighbors' papers if something good comes out about "those Vols" that he wants to share in three states. He sent a safety article about pickup trucks to the eighteen-year-old who received the transportation vehicle of his dreams for his birthday.

Our youngest ones are still interested in baby animals, so every time the zoo has a new arrival, we send the article and a made-up birth announcement. Their telephone calls often begin with: "What's new at the zoo?"

One day at work (don't tell my boss) I copied my hand on the Xerox machine and dropped a note to the one who had the measles. Next week, we received a shot of Raggedy Ann, made on Dad's Xerox!

Camcorders have taken the place of many cameras, and digital cameras now make some of our old pictures look ancient. But we still use our old stand-by. Our Grandchildren have more photographs of our dogs, Dolly and Benson, than they do of their own pets. When Paul came to visit one time, he asked, "Can Benson be my dog while I am here?"

They take vacations with us through our snapshots. They watch our garden grow from beginning to fruition. Those in warmer climates all enjoyed the snow at our house through pictures. When Grampa Kenny came out of surgery one time, his first question was, "Did you bring the camera? I want this to be seen!"

Be sharing of your lives and your never-ending love, your Grandchildren will feel the depth of your caring, for *love* can't be bought with a present.

Q: We had never seen one of our Grandchildren and were so afraid that he would never get to know us. We lived too far away and wanted him to really understand us as people who loved him.

We made cassettes of us reading stories, singing, and telling about all of our days' activities. I even told him about my trips to the grocery! We wanted him to recognize our voices and also know what we would have told him in person.

His mother said he would take his little tape player to bed with him every night and listen to our voices. She said he practically wore some of them out.

We finally moved to Columbia, South Carolina, to be nearer them and now have followed them to Cookeville. But we are not moving anymore!

We have a great relationship with this Grandson and feel the early tapes have made the difference.

The rest of our Grandchildren already lived in the Middle Tennessee area, so we now are able to be Grandparents to all of them.

Marjorie, Cookeville

Dear Marjorie,

I have visions of this little fellow curled up in bed with the loving voices of his Grandparents singing him off to sleep. This is an idea we could all put to use. I have suggested before reading books on tape for your Grandchildren, but the idea of singing, even if it is not star quality, sounds harmonious to a child.

Long-distance Grandparenting can be a lot of fun and very challenging. GaMe Marion tells me she spends as much on stamps as she would on a toy and never feels guilty. Her letters and cards are the way she maintains a close connection.

Q: *We have a Grandchild that is handicapped and we love her very much. She lives in another state and we wanted to know how to encourage and love her without adding to her everyday stress. After asking our daughter how to best handle our communication with her, she sent a booklet from her therapist. I thought part of what we have learned might be helpful to others.*

Connecting with special Grandchildren at long distance does not require any additional talent, but we have to keep in mind the following guidelines: at the top of the list is our acceptance of the specialness of our Granddaughter and her unique limitations and gifts. We are sensitive to her special needs in our letters, stories, and presents. We never patronize her.

We try never to put her in a position that will make her feel frustrated and inadequate. For example, she has difficulty reading and we know better than to send her sophisticated books and stories. She also has difficulties with coordination, so we are always on the lookout for toys and gifts that do not require a lot of dexterity.

We would never want to add stress to her life by insisting she do more than she is capable. We tread the path between acceptance and greater expectations.

We are constantly reading and researching about her disability. We know that the more information we can accumulate, the better we are equipped to handle her needs.

We are constantly sending her letters that her mother reads to her, books on her level, and pictures of animals. Any other suggestions?

Janie, Old Hickory

Dear Janie,

I think you could be teaching a workshop to a lot of us about people in general. I am sure there are many Grandparents out there who will benefit from your experiences.

I might add, if there are other Grandchildren living in this same family, that ways might be found to insure they feel "special" as well. Often, a child that is sick or has other problems becomes the focus of the family and the other children will begin to resent that.

Q: I recently relocated to Nashville and wanted to share an idea with your readers that may be of help to long-distance Grandparents.

I was at the birth of my Grandson and babysat for him every two or three weekends since he was a week old. This close relationship had gone on for the past four-and-a-half years until I had to leave Iowa and this precious gift.

I was a mess trying to figure out a way to stay close to my best boy and make the transition easier on both of us.

After lots of thinking, I came up with the perfect idea. I buy books for Cody, tape record me reading them to him along with a message at the end of each story such as, "Remember even though we can't be together, Grandma always loves you, no matter what." After I have recorded a tape (which holds five to six stories, depending on book length), I send the tape along with the books to Cody. He loves to have Mommy read him a bedtime story every night and then he gets to have Gramma tuck him in with a taped bedtime story after that.

Sometimes when I feel really creative, I'll make up the stories that I record along with a handwritten book. If you do that, be sure and keep a copy because sometimes they may ask about the story and if you don't get it right, they will tell you about it!

I know the idea is a success at my daughter's house because now when I call and talk to Cody, every once in a while he says, "I need more stories, Gramma!" It's a small cost to be able to remain an active part of a wonderful little boy's life and remind him he is always loved even though we can't be together as often. It doesn't take much time and it is lots of fun, too!

Kerry, Antioch

Dear Kerry,

Cody certainly is a lucky fellow! These tapes will remain a family keepsake and he will probably play them for his children. Thanks for the warm and cuddly idea.

Q: My husband and I recently moved to Middle Tennessee with our twenty-month-old daughter. Before, we were close enough to her Grandparents to see them regularly, but now there are more than two hundred extra miles between us. This makes visits with my mother (who is now an eight-hour drive away) especially difficult. Other than lots of phone calls and pictures, can you offer suggestions for ways to make sure the Grandparents feel involved in our daughter's life? They miss her terribly and count the weeks between visits.

Renita, Clarksville

Dear Renita,

One of my favorite suggestions to Grandparents is to send tape-recorded bedtime stories, so you could also be making tapes of your daughter as she utters those new cutesy words and rambling endearing sentences.

As Grandparents can send sing-along tapes, maybe you and your daughter could begin singing and make her first tapes. Of course, Camcorders are staple items in most young households and any activity tapes will be wonderful to send. Friends tell me that the videos taken on their own visit with their Grandchildren are some of the best repeat movies at their house.

You can ask your parents to send pictures and stories of various family members, and then during the next personal visit, your daughter will be able to relate the stories and names back to them.

A very simple way to keep your parents involved is to keep a daily diary of your daughter's adventures and changes. Describe your community, moving adjustments, and new friends to the Grandparents. This type of weekly newsletter can be very meaningful to other parents who are dealing with the hardship of long-distance visits.

The important part of this relationship is communication in any form. Cell phones now make for a less expensive way to keep in touch, but for the economical price of a stamp, many occasions can be recorded for the joy and lifetime value to a Grandparent.

Enjoy the experiences.

Q: I wrote to you two-and-a-half years ago when my husband, daughter, and I first moved away from our families to the area. I asked for ways to make sure that my daughter stayed close to her Grandparents. Our daughter has just turned four, and we also have a nine-month-old daughter. Any fears I had about them not knowing their Grandparents are gone.

Through phone conversations and greeting cards that arrive for no reason (often with a stick of gum or some stickers) both my daughters know their Grandparents love and think of them often. One thing my mother did to help stay in touch with Maryn, our older daughter, was to give her a plastic mailbox, which sits outside Maryn's playhouse. I put letters in there from her Grandparents. She knows to look for her mail when the flag is up.

My mother-in-law has stopped working and is now able to visit more often. Maryn is even comfortable enough with her to go to her home for a week, with only a twinge of homesickness.

I wanted to share a story that illustrates just how close a child can be to her Grandparents, even when they're hours apart.

Recently, Maryn asked me what Granddaddy, Nana, and Aunt Kathy were doing. "Well, Granddaddy and Aunt Kathy are at work and Nana— What do you think Nana is probably doing right now?"

"Standing around doing nothing," she answered.

"Why do you think that?" I surprisingly asked.

"Because I'm not there!"

Thanks for encouraging me to keep up communication and know that life would move on in a positive way.

Renita, Murfreesboro

Dear Renita,

What a wonderful story. All Grandparents should be so lucky to think their Grandchildren see them as that devoted.

You are right in that staying in touch can be as simple as a stick of gum, but I really like the mailbox idea.

Suzanne, our daughter, has her first Grandchild who lives in Colorado. She has begun to tape stories of favorite books and send the tape and book to Zac. At the beginning she tells him that when she makes a sound like a train, that is the time to turn the page. I am not sure who is having more fun with this project, but they are both feeling very connected.

TRAVEL

Q: Even though I am not a Grandparent yet, I regularly read your column. I wanted to add something I believe to be valuable about traveling with Grandchildren.

Please encourage Grandparents to have proper identification for their Grandchildren before they take them on car trips. One of my worries as a parent is that my caregiver or in-laws would have an accident and the emergency personnel would not know to whom the children belonged. I keep this identification in my own wallet, as well, for the same reason.

There are three things Grandparents need to have: a copy of each child's insurance card, a letter from the parents authorizing the Grandparents to have treatment done, and a photo ID for each child. Photo IDs for children over the age of one can be obtained from the driver's license bureau with a birth certificate and social security card.

I purchased clear plastic covers used for baseball cards and inserted the insurance card, letter, and ID with the picture showing. I made several copies and gave them to each Grandparent and have them for anyone babysitting. I keep mine in my wallet with my own ID so that emergency personnel can find them easily.

Please pass this information on. It could save hours of confusion.

Denise, Tullahoma

Dear Denise,

If I could give a prize—you should win the Tip of the Year!

Thanks for the reminder. The same situation happened to a cousin traveling with their Granddaughter. She developed a virus and had to be taken to an emergency room. The time it took to find the parents, get approval, and treat the child was hours beyond the standard waiting time.

Parents should take this advice to heart and immediately prepare the packets you suggested for each child that might be in a car with Grandparents or caretakers. Be sure and include phone numbers for parents at work.

Q: I read and enjoy your column regularly. I have pondered the following situation until I'm afraid that I am becoming obsessed about it. My husband and I have invited our youngest Granddaughter, Jessica, age twelve, to join us on a trip to St. Maarten during her spring break. We will be staying for one week in a resort and taking side trips.

My concern is not allowing Jessica enough freedom. I cannot imagine even wanting her to go to the drink machine without one of us watching. She is a very mature, reliable young lady and will be a pleasure to have on the trip, but I can just imagine someone snatching her (she's also very beautiful) and something awful happening.

I realize that I read too many current events to be relaxed about this, but I do want her to have a wonderful time and happy memories. Can you please react to this paranoid Nana? Thanks.

Ann, (e-mail)

Dear Ann,

I think I would be as paranoid as you are. We do not live in a safe world anymore. We have to be constantly alert for ourselves and, therefore, it is imperative that we are protective of the Grandchildren we are entertaining.

A twelve-year-old can be mature and reliable, but still inexperienced with situations and people of the world. I would talk to her about your concerns, your responsibilities as the adult in this locality, and have a three-way discussion on what method and procedures everyone can agree on, in order to remain safely together and still have good times.

My first thought was that all of you have proper identification on you at all times and that you carry a phone number of your resort. Don't forget to take a consent form from the parents, in case you need medical treatment for your Granddaughter.

Her parents apparently feel safe about you taking their daughter, so I would enjoy the time together. Try to put all those fears just below the surface, for no one will have a good time if you are in a panic every minute about your surroundings.

Wish we were going with you!

Q: We have a travel trailer and are planning on taking two of our Grandchildren on a three-week trip through the West. They are ten- and twelve-years-old, and have never been gone this long from their parents. Do you have any special advice?

Cinda, Columbia

Dear Cinda,

Number one is to make sure your vitamins are packed in a water-proof bag and you are totally relaxed! I applaud your desire to entertain for this length of time and suggest you call home at night. This keeps Mother and Daddy calm.

Make sure you have all the proper information and release forms. (Note previous articles.)

You will be doing a lot of traveling, but make time for rest and relaxation. You don't want your days to be so action-packed that everyone is totally exhausted by bedtime. Plan nap time into your schedule. This includes the Grandchildren!

Set up behavior standards before you leave. It is no time to set rules once the trip has begun. Maintaining a litter-free earth and remembering the rules their parents have taught are good guidelines.

Travel-trailer parks will also have different circumstances than a trip on Amtrak or a cruise around the open seas. Make sure your Grandchildren understand the standard rules of safety and "staying within sight."

Talk about the places you will eat. Will you be cooking all the time, or will you be visiting some fancy restaurants? Allow the children to help with making menus and selecting various cuisines.

Budgets and money should also be addressed, with the amount to be spent on souvenirs determined ahead of time.

Have a good time, take lots of pictures, and bring home lots of memorabilia.

Q: We have decided to take our twin Granddaughters (six years old) on a long weekend trip. We know they will get restless and tired of the five-hour drive we have planned. Any suggestions?

Martin, Shelbyville

Dear Martin,

Put a large towel, quilt, or bedspread on the backseat. Pack a cooler and plenty of snacks.

Create a surprise package for each girl. It will be wise to have identical goodies in each bag. Fill these with small games or toys. There are many games now for travel that have magnetic boards and playing pieces.

Hand puppets are good for car travel. Dolls with lots of change-able clothes can keep little girls busy for a long time.

Etch-a-Sketch will occupy some people for many hours. Hand-held computer games for this age and fabric versions of tic-tac-toe will help them pass the miles.

Buy inexpensive binoculars and give them the job of finding objects as you travel down the road.

Bring a tape player and learn some new songs. Our youngest Grandchildren, Hayden and Audrey, can sing the same songs for at least an hour without getting tired.

Create stories. You begin with the characters and plot and let the twins add to the story line. Keep the fantasies going as long as it is funny and interesting.

Little girls might enjoy stringing large beads and making neck-laces out of prepackaged boxes you have stashed away. Lap trays will let them color or look at books.

You might plan on taking portable horseshoe or miniature golf sets to play with at the rest stops. This allows them to get rid of some of that energy without getting too far from your designated space.

To keep the eternal question from being asked forty thousand times, make a map of your trip. Laminate it and let them follow along with a magic marker. Make sure you have highlighted several objects and towns to anticipate as they travel along.

Pack their favorite pillow and blankie—in case they do get sleepy! Have disposable face and hand wipes, trash baggies, and plenty of patience. Double up on your vitamins and enjoy the trip.

Q: *In a recent column, you wrote about preparing Granddaughters for a long auto trip. I think you missed an opportunity to talk about healthful*

snacks. I see so many obese children (who grow up to be like the many obese adults I see).

Since children will be storing up unexpended energy on an auto trip, they certainly don't need to add sugar to their diet, in any form. I would have suggested a raw apple, a small bunch of grapes, or a banana (all of these have natural sugars). I would also point out the importance of not offering soft drinks of any kind. I think water is the only acceptable drink on this kind of trip, and it is the only drink which quenches the thirst. I might also add that, in my opinion, milk and water are the only acceptable drinks for children at any time.

I grew up not knowing that people snacked in between meals. I was shocked when I saw this for the first time. I thought, "What is she doing eating at this time of day?" I realize this may have been unusual. My own children were brought up the same way. I am not saying that everyone has to do as I did though. But look around you at the results of all the fast foods, sugary snacks, and carbonated drinks.

I am a mother of five and a Grandmother of eleven.

Mamie, Portland

Dear Mamie,

Your theory and philosophy are great, and if the Grandchildren basically have the wonderful nutritional practices you describe, by all means keep up the good work.

Many children also have food allergies or food intolerance, and as caring baby-sitters, we should always respect and conform to the necessary precautions.

I don't feel it is my job to force children to like apples and broccoli when they have been living on pizza and ice cream.

I agree that we should *try* to keep young people eating healthy, but when children, who are allowed to eat anything at anytime, come to visit and we attempt to change their eating habits in one swoop— they will not want to make that trip again.

Q: I thought you might be interested in some activities from a silly Grandmother. On a recent cruise to Alaska, I saved ship boarding passes, luggage tickets, covers for beverage glasses, room service menus, laundry bags, and other items in the goody bag provided in our stateroom.

The day following our arrival home, with suitcases still on the bedroom floor, containing accessories (shoes, shawls, hats, bathing suits, jewelry, etc.) three Granddaughters, ages four, two, and three months, were invited to a "cruise party." They tagged their luggage, then proceeded to pack (more shoes, T-shirts, etc.) from my closet and rolled their suitcases through the house before using boarding passes to get on ship as I became the cruise director.

We took binoculars in the living room to look out of windows for whales and dolphins (the four-year-old's vivid imagination spotted several).

They proceeded to strip and put on my bathing suits for a pretend swim in the "ship's solarium." Hilarious sight, needless to say!

Afterwards, they ordered room service. I served orange juice and crackers on a silver tray to their stateroom.

Next, they dressed to the hilt for the captain's gala in jewelry, scarves, shawls, party shoes, and purses.

Shopping onshore for souvenirs was last, and they chose from the assorted key chains, etc., putting them in their shopping bags as we returned to ship.

The party lasted about an hour, the girls really got into the spirit of it, and I had fun propped up on the bed, loving on the three-month-old, while carrying out my duties as cruise director.

The trip to Alaska was most enjoyable, but the cruise party trip almost surpassed it.

Dorothy, Nashville

Dear Dorothy,

What a vivid way to show your Grandchildren what you had been doing. I have delightful images of how all this took place in your home. This is probably just the beginning of trips they will remember!

I saw a cartoon last week depicting a Grandmother wrapped in a straitjacket to restrain her from buying stuff for her Grandchildren. If we could all realize that our time and personal attention mean so much more to them.

These are some examples of the difference in the Grandparents of today. We are not quiet, cookie-baking *old* people. We are vivacious, busy, energetic people, interested in the world, and anxious to share some of this vitality with Grandchildren.

I want to relate my vacation trip with my Granddaughters. We were gone three weeks and camped all across the Northwest.

We started in Chicago, where one of them lives, and slept in tents every night thereafter. We cooked over an open fire with the simplest of utensils and bathed in campground facilities.

A wonderful experience. I only hope I am able to do this again next year.

Benna, Knoxville

Couldn't wait to tell you about my experience at my Grandson's wedding. They planned the ceremony in Jamaica, so that everyone could have a special vacation together.

One of Granny's thrills was para-skiing over the Caribbean. I am seventy and have started a list of all the adventures I want to encounter before I sit back to rock!

I understand my Grandchildren are sending me up in a hot-air balloon for my birthday next month!

Peg, Memphis

I read all of your columns and thought I would make a small suggestion to traveling with kids. Portable TV/VCR/DVD players are all available and most children are accustomed to this type entertainment. I know it sounds like a form of "just keeping the kids quiet," but if you have traveled a lot with three rambunctious boys, you would want some quiet time.

Karla, Crossville

As a Grandparent who travels a lot with the Elderhostel program, I also take advantage of their Intergenerational Weeks. For those who don't know,

Elderhostel provides educational and active weeks for people over fifty-five years old. I have been to seven states, rafted down the Colorado River, traveled to Ireland, and ridden a train across Canada. I have taken my Grandchildren on a week of crafts in North Carolina and another week touring Nova Scotia.

Martha, McMinnville

HOLIDAYS

Q: *Our Grandsons, ages six and eight, from another state are coming to spend a week after Christmas. Their parents will be here also. I am thrilled to have them, but dread the noise and confusion. My son allows them to completely run undisciplined. They go to bed when they want and eat at all hours.*

The children can be very sweet when they are alone, but when their parents are around, they have different personalities,

I am not a confronter, so don't suggest I say something to my son. I am too old to get in arguments over how to raise children. I just pray they will grow up someday and live productive lives.

Now, do you have any suggestions that might make my time less stressful?

Peaceful Granny, Franklin

Dear Granny,

There are lots of Grandparents just like you—those who prefer harmony at whatever price.

A therapist recently suggested "visualize a peaceful, quiet visit when you are expecting company and the stress will be less."

While you are "visualizing," make plans to do something alone with the boys. Go to a movie or museum, take them to their favorite fast-food restaurant, or just walk through a park. You will be in complete control while you become more acquainted with your Grandchildren.

You might explain to them that noise and running gives you a headache and could they help you keep everyone else quiet. They are old enough to feel responsible toward helping protect your health. When you notice them playing quietly, compliment them on their support.

Announce to the entire household what time you go to bed (maybe even set it earlier than normal) and close your door at that time. They may take the hint. If not, you will still be able to have quiet time.

Plan one meal a day that will be served at ___o'clock and stick to it. Have plenty of breakfast and sandwich foods for them to eat whenever they are hungry.

Set some limits for yourself and this will make you feel a little bit in charge of the visit.

Keep reminding yourself this is a family holiday you want to be successful and it will be over in only seven days.

They will grow up and only remember your love.

Q: *You cannot imagine how I dread holidays. My mother makes it impossible. I think she just lives to make everyone else miserable. She has treated us this way all of our lives.*

Our Thanksgiving was ruined by her negative comments on the food, what we wore, and how my house looked. She can be a very nice lady to strangers, but to her family she is awful.

A friend suggested we just not include her in our dinners, but that seems like a drastic way to go, although I would love to have a holiday that was peaceful and loving.

By the way, she lives one hundred miles from us, has a kind husband (my stepfather), and another daughter where she lives.

Aching for Peace, Celina

Dear Aching,

To those people who grow up with loving and devoted parents, they can't believe that your situation exists. To those other thousands who have a parent that is similar to yours, or worse, there is a book that I highly recommend.

In Joyce Landorf Heatherley's *Irregular People*, she writes: "they are the ones who have the knack of wounding you every time you see them. They say the wrong thing, they ruin your day, and they keep your emotions in constant turmoil. You can't reason with them, can't depend on them and can't expect any real support from them."

She goes on to say this is usually not a friend that you can run away from, but a family member who must be dealt with on some kind of continuing basis.

Joyce acknowledges that there are no simple solutions to the irregular person problem, and that any kind of relationship may often be filled with heartache.

I suggest you weigh the outcome of cutting your mother off from holidays or putting up with her. Which decision can you live with? Which choice will be most beneficial to your family? How dramatically will she react to this decision? Will that make you feel worse? Why isn't she staying home with your sister?

Plan a different kind of holiday. Take a trip, visit some other family members, or find some other way to spend this occasion without Mama.

Q: *My Grandmother is coming to visit in April. She came last year and spent the week of Easter with us. We had a good time, but I hated her cooking. She wanted us to eat all these greasy casseroles. She got mad because we didn't like them. We don't eat much meat at our house and that is all she cooks. Lots of times we didn't even know what all she put in those dishes.*

My brother and I don't want to hurt her feelings or make her mad at us, but we are already dreading the cooking part of her visit.

She sends me your column sometimes when she wants to make a point that we disagree on! I hope you can help us, but please don't tell us to buck up and eat her cooking.

Desperate, (e-mail)

Dear Desperate,

I appreciate the fact that you don't want to upset your Grandmother and that you want to continue to develop a growing relationship. I wouldn't dare try to tell you what to eat!

Sometimes Grandmothers go by the rule that the way to someone's heart is through their stomach. Maybe your mother can already have meals planned and ready to prepare while she is there, so that you will have time to be together in more places than the kitchen. You and your brother might even show off your kitchen skills by finishing up one of these pre-planned meals.

You could also ask her to tell you about some of her favorite dessert recipes. I am sure there will be something you would enjoy from her many years of experienced cooking. I can't believe there will not be wonderful goodies on her list. My Grandmothers cooked like yours and I only remember the tea cakes that would melt in my mouth.

Select one dessert that sounds good to you, write down her instructions, and then prepare it together.

Giving her a speech on the perils of eating too much meat and fat will probably fall on deaf ears. If you have had any lessons on nutrition in school, you might pull those out and ask her to help you with an assignment, even if you completed it ten months ago. This would give you an opportunity to discuss eating healthy.

Good Luck!

Q: *Help! Thanksgiving was a disaster at our house. My son's new wife and her three children did not get along with my daughter's children. They all fought, whined, or pouted all day.*

My husband said he was leaving home for Christmas. What am I going to do?
Panicky, Lafayette

Dear Panicky,

Well, well, well! As if we didn't have enough stress during the holidays—along comes something else.

Some marketing wizard declared Thanksgiving as the "shopping-est" weekend of the year and now his, mine, ours, and theirs are suppose to sit down together and automatically "love one another."

We have never asked our five grown children (blended through marriage) to come together for Christmas. They have all cooperated superbly for family reunions and birthdays, but a gift to us—and them—has been to try and enjoy each family individually. A weekend, a day, or a dinner, whatever time allows, has been set aside for personal Peace on Earth.

Don't let worn-out traditions dictate what should be happening at your house. The world has changed so drastically, we should be able to back up and take a look at what is really important in our lives. Young children grow up quickly. We need to help them slow down and hear the songs of harmony and tranquility.

Begin new traditions that all your Grandchildren will remember. One Granny (who has moved to a condo) takes each of her Grandchildren—one at a time—to a restaurant of his or her choosing before Christmas for private giggles and opening of inexpensive gifts. She says this allows them to have her undivided attention and gives her the pleasure of enjoying the uniqueness of each child.

There is the story of the devoted mother who had so many children, she often took her apron and covered her head for some quiet time. She must have later taken that same apron and pulled a single child under with her to give them exclusive calmness.

The wonderful image of having everyone together rarely meets with reality! Make the time for individual visits with your families.

Q: I am really annoyed at my oldest daughter. For all my children's lives, we have been having Easter together at our house. This year she has too many other commitments to come. Trivial things to me—friend's birthday and ball practice for her sons.

We feel that family is more important than outside activities, but we want to be understanding of their schedules. It just seems that they should put their parents ahead of other appointments.

Our other daughters will be here. What should I say for next year?

Carol, Milan

Dear Carol,

My mother's ghost must be unusually astute today, for I can hear myself (several years ago) saying, "Mother and Daddy don't have anything else to do. Why can't they come to our house instead of us having to pack up two boys and go to them?"

Now that I am a Grandparent, I feel the same as you, but . . .

Grandparents today have a tremendous advantage. Unless we are working too hard or have extreme health problems, we have very few restrictions on how we chart our calendar.

I also have had occasions to wonder why that event was more important than what we planned, but I refused to let it affect my festivities. Many people would suggest you confront your daughter and tell her of your hurt feelings. Others agree with me that allowing everyone to do what is best for them saves hurt feelings.

I was an only child and that made a vast difference. We now have five children and rarely are they all together at one time. If we get four out of five couples (not even beginning to count all the Grandchildren), we consider that a monumental miracle. We try desperately to work around their schedules and accept their company when they can come and go to them when they plan a special time for us.

Find another time to visit with your daughter. You have been fortunate if you have managed to get all three families together until now. Why not let the three girls decide when and where for next time?

Be open and adaptable. Life is too short to be rigid.

Q: I just spent a miserable Thanksgiving with three of our Grandchildren. I don't want to blame them for their behavior, but cannot imagine my daughter allowing this type of conduct.

They were loud, demanding, and had no table manners. They refused to sit at the table, but would eat a bite or two standing up and then go play or race out the door and ride their new scooters. I politely asked them if they would like some cake or ice cream for dessert, and they laughed at me. "We don't want your stuff. Mom brought our favorite candy."

My daughter simply ignored them. Her husband would occasionally tell them to slow down or not to slam the door.

Before you ask, they belong to both of them. They birthed these little monsters. The oldest is ten and the youngest is six.

I cannot imagine how they survive in school. Although they go to private school, they have now been to three different ones.

They had not visited our home in four years and, at that time, everything was fairly normal. Now, they have moved closer and announced they would see us on Christmas Day.

I don't believe that I can deal with this type of conduct. Can I tell them they must behave and use manners while they are in my home?

Upset, Carthage

Dear Upset,

First of all, I don't think telling these children to behave will have much effect. Unless you are a very strong, assertive Grandparent, I would probably suggest that you keep your thoughts to yourself temporarily. Your daughter and her husband have allowed this to happen because they do not want the rigors of discipline or, by some mistaken theory, feel the children should express their individuality.

I would "invite" myself to their house for Christmas. You could say, "Because I know how difficult it will be for the children to leave their new toys."

After the holidays, you might want to sit down with your daughter and explain your concerns and feelings. She may get mad and threaten to never bring them back. You must then give in or stand your ground.

Check out Drs. Cloud and Townsend's book *Boundaries*.

Q: Our daughter has invited us to visit them for Easter. They live in another state and we know they have been having financial problems. We do not want

to impose any more burdens on them by our visit, but they truly seem to want us to come. We know the additional meals and miscellaneous things will cost extra.

They have mentioned several short sightseeing trips they have planned, and we really want to help with these expenses. How do we go about it without it becoming embarrassing to them or us?

Loving Mother, Celina

Dear Loving Mother,

They may have been saving up for this visit. It may be a sacrifice they are happily willing to make, or they may expect you to help out some when you get there.

It is often difficult to know what to do about financial aid to your children. Unless they have children, I normally don't recommend giving them money.

I often remember early married days when we had a limited budget. My daddy would occasionally send me a check with, "Had a little extra and wanted to share it with you." I think in their later years they felt that we paid them back in other ways.

You also have the option of phoning your daughter and asking what expenses you can help with. She may argue a little, but you can point out that you really want to help out monetarily with this visit.

Another alternative is to go, see the lay of the land, and play it by ear. You can offer to pay for tickets to some of this sightseeing or take them out to eat or just give your daughter some money. (A check is good, for then she can turn down the offer by not cashing it.)

The important thing is being together and communicating. Enjoy their life and don't worry so much!

Q: My Grandchildren are coming to visit for the first time in my new condominium. I am very anxious to have them, but I do have a lot of antiques and sentimental knickknacks. I don't want to be constantly in fear of their breaking

things, neither do I want to be a nag with, "Don't touch that," every minute.

I can't see putting all these things away while they are here. How do other Grandparents handle this?

Norma, Memphis

Dear Norma,

When my Grandchildren started coming for visits, I got a cardboard box (you can get a fancy storage box at most all the stores today) and filled it with items to keep them busy.

I bought coloring books, lots of crayons, paints, books, and games. When I did my yard sale shopping, I was always on the alert for something new in their eyes. Over the years, the box is the first thing they pull out when they come in and rarely are they interested in my personal things. Over the years, they have added to the box by leaving items behind.

One Granny told of creating a tree house on her carpeted stairs for bears and stuffed animals. She says the steps have now become condominiums for Barbie and Ken and My Little Ponies.

Hazel turned a walk-in closet into a play house for Jenny. She even wants to sleep in there when she stays overnight. All her toys are kept in there and she can bring them out to play, but always puts them back. She is even allowed to have snack time in her playhouse.

Pearl always used a coffee table covered with a quilt and that became a safe place for Autumn to play on. Naturally she kept all of her secret stuff under the coffee table and would often hide there. One day, Pearl found her asleep under the coffee table.

Distractions of their own interests will leave them very little time for curiosity about your things. If they understand what the priceless items are, where they came from, and "someday when you are all grown up, this will be yours," they develop their own sense of responsibility about your possessions.

If all this doesn't work or if you just can't be comfortable about your things, then pack them away in the closet. Someday, you will realize time spent with your Grandchildren is so much more important.

Q: Now that summer is here, we are looking forward to our Grandchildren coming for visits.

They are growing up and probably will need different forms of entertainment. Do you have any ideas on special projects for the summer?

Olivia, Fairfield Glade

Dear Olivia,

As you know, we all learn more from experience than reading about it in a book, or newspaper column. My concepts for summer were quickly converted last week when eight-year-old Jessica spent a few days.

I had assumed rented videos would be a focal point for her afternoon quiet time. No! She had seen everything in the video shop and was dismayed at how few "really awesome" movies we had seen. She made us a long list of all we really "had" to see.

My plans in the kitchen are always a much anticipated event, but this time she had lessons for me. "Don't you know you can cook spaghetti in the microwave? Just break it up in a big bowl of water, add salt, pepper, and cook for 12 minutes!"

She was right. That sure did beat standing over the stove. I am constantly amazed at how much our Grandchildren can teach us.

She also decided she wanted to help plant our spring garden. She very meticulously dropped the beans in the row. "I don't know how you did this without me before. Now, I will have to come back every year at this time." Most children love to grow things. Even if they can't stay to see them grown. You can mail photos of the completed project.

After she had picked a handful of clover for Grampa Kenny, he showed her how we made bracelets and necklaces from the blossoms when we were her age. We were pleased and she reacted as if she had redesigned the Barbie doll.

We decided when there is nothing new to do, go back to the old things that worked for us when we were young. Believe it or not, they do want to hear what you did as a youngster. Jessica loved checkers and sitting on an old quilt out in the yard.

If the videos and computer games lose their interest, try some simple outdoor activities.

Q: My eight-year-old Granddaughter just spent a wonderful week at our house. We took her on several short trips, let her stay up late, and planned menus at her request. It was our first time to keep her and we thought it went fabulous.

After she got home we received a note from her mother. My husband and I were excited about opening the letter, expecting to hear good things about our Granddaughter's visit. Much to our surprise, it was a scathing letter of how we spoiled her and that she could never come back again.

We have no idea on how to respond to this.

Frustrated, Buffalo Valley

Dear Frustrated,

For a very long time, I have been saying, "When the children are at our house, they live by our rules and receive special treatment." That sounds good for most Grandparents, but a couple of months ago, I was in a group of young mothers, of which two could have been your daughter-in-law. They were angry at the Grandparents for spoiling their children.

One had a strong-willed seven-year-old. "I had spent one hour every night for six months talking, calming, and teaching him how to take the time to think before he acts. He ended up the school year with his first satisfactory in behavior. His Grandparents wiped that out in one short week by their permissiveness!"

The other mother had a hyper-child, brought on by some food allergies. The Grandparents had disregarded her reminders and the child returned home bouncing off the walls.

Amendment to my thinking! Ask if there are any special things we should be cautious about: food allergies, too much activity, tendency to_____, etc. As Grandparents we should be helping to properly guide these angels, but first we have to know which predicaments the parents are dealing with at the time.

I suggest you write (a phone call can too often become an argument) your daughter-in-law and describe your wonderful week. Apologize for causing any confusion to your Granddaughter and, "Next time before she visits, you and I can sit down and work out some of the rules I need to remember."

Stay nice to your daughter-in-law! You never know when she is the only person standing between you and your Grandchildren.

Q: *I wanted to have my two Grandsons visit together this summer. One lives in Atlanta and the other one lives in Memphis. I felt they needed the chance to get better acquainted.*

Their stay was a disaster! They fought the entire time they were together. It was almost as if they came with their minds set on not liking each other.

Their mothers are my two only daughters and they have always gotten along well—until they married. Now, they seem to argue all the time about nothing important.

I wanted their children to be close. What did I do wrong? What can I do to help?
Shirley, Rockwood

Dear Shirley,

Remember the old saying, "We can pick our friends, but our family is selected automatically?" This is something we all often forget.

Your daughters may have secretly had problems growing up that you didn't notice, or maybe their marriage has made them jealous of what the other has acquired.

All of this has rubbed off on your Grandsons as they are hearing comments at home. They may have come with preconceived notions of each other that one visit is not going to correct.

You should probably wait until they are older and try again. In the meantime, you just can't make people like each other. We are all too unique.

My advice on vacationing with Grandchildren: whenever possible, take them one at a time.

These visits give you the opportunity to see and understand the whole child. They have the center stage. Their personality is unaffected by an audience of their peers. They will talk about topics they would never discuss in front of others.

We have learned over the years that only one Grandchild per visit is the way for all of us to really communicate, get acquainted, and do what we each like to do. Amanda wanted to sing and perform, Jessica wanted to cook and prowl. Now Audrey wants to do fourteen things in one hour, but her favorite is still painting nails.

Q: I read all these letters to you about Grandparents who have such a terrible time when they visit their kids. Why don't they just stay in a motel?

That physical separation at night can be invaluable in dealing with the next day. They could even throw a sleepover with the kids, individually, or together if they can handle it, providing the parents a night alone in their own home.

If they do this, I would suggest that they choose to express some aspect of the truth: "As we grow older, we find that we increasingly value our privacy and quiet time. I know that staying at a motel may not make sense to you since we came to visit you, but that little bit of time alone at the motel really gives us time to relax. I hope you can respect that."

Then Grandparents need to stick to that explanation, without elaboration.

Whether they stay at a motel or not, I would suggest that they have some individual time with each Grandchild. These dates, such as time at the park on the swings or a trip to a museum, can be very important in forming a child's feel of self-worth, and in their forming an individual relationship with the child while they are young.

The individual relationships are where the value comes from. In addition, it gives them a break from the overwhelming noisy situations in the home, while achieving their goal of spending time with the Grandchildren.

Wanda, Sewanee

Dear Wanda,

You have made several important suggestions, but I can't imagine any of our children understanding our wanting to stay at a motel. Although, they all live within one hundred miles and if we don't choose to stay all night, we just go back home.

I am hearing more and more of Grandparents that do choose to stay in a nearby hotel or motel. We all need our rest! We all need our nightly habits! We all like our own routines! Your idea would work for lots of people.

Chapter 4

THE GIFT OF LOVE

Is It All About Money?

GRANDPARENTS COME IN ALL SIZES, SHAPES, AND opinions. If you don't believe that theory, ask the next ten you know about their view of baby-sitting!

While grocery shopping last week, a woman wheeled up beside me and announced, "You are the Grandparent Lady! I want you to write a column about not feeling guilty when you don't want to baby-sit! I have spent all summer taking care of my Grandchildren and I am too old for this stuff. We have had each one individually and spent all of our time entertaining. I guess you already know—most of them don't believe in naps. I need my afternoon nap!"

She barely paused to say, "I love all of them, but I do have another life. I don't want to feel guilty for spending some time by myself!"

As she wheeled out of sight, she turned back to say, "If you need any more quotes, you can call me," and returned to scribble her number on the top of my Frosted Mini-Wheat's box.

The next day this original poem came from Margaret Patton of Goodlettsville. She explained her Grandchildren and their parents had just moved to another state.

Oh, how quiet it is this morning when Granny comes down the stairs. Not any toys, games or even GI Joe's to watch for.

Oh how quiet it is, not any little Grandchildren asking for a bowl of cereal, not any half glasses of milk from the night before, not any good morning hugs and kisses, just an empty kitchen.

Oh, how quiet it is, how lonely it is when the Grandchildren are gone. Is this really life?

Grandparents should have the decision on how much visiting is "just right." Many do not have that option! They are rearing their own Grandchildren. Most of us can decide when to send them home.

Personally, I like them better after they can talk, feed themselves, and go to the bathroom in the proper place! I really enjoy the ones who still think I know marvelous secrets, am young at heart, and can sing the songs they know.

Then there are those wonderful young-adult Grandchildren. They are truly the heart of my life. They come and go at everyone's leisure and readily ask for advice, thank you for being there, and making the world a better place.

Grandparenting is fun—especially when you can choose the time and quantity!

Q: I have agreed to pick up my four-year-old Granddaughter after preschool this fall and am having second thoughts. It seems that all she does is argue, stomp her foot, and shout, "no!" I thought the terrible twos were supposed to be the hardest time, but she seems to be getting worse.

So do you have any suggestions for me?

Nana, Livingston

Dear Nana,

I am not sure the terrible twos end at that time. It seems that three and four can be very difficult for parents and children, therefore baby-sitting Grandparents are left to feel somehow responsible for changing their personality.

Try to remember that is just a time of asserting a budding individuality. She is telling everyone that she is ready "to do it myself." She is announcing to everyone that she is very self-assured, able, and wonderful. This will often come across as being too independent, but she is learning.

You can help her by being patient as she grows and stretches. Recognize that her actions are a way of development. Avoid some of her power struggles by not arguing, but simply taking hold of her hand and leading her where you wanted her to go.

Maintain a sense of humor. Children can be in such conflict with what they want. I always laugh when I see teenagers struggling to be different by all wearing the same outfit.

Don't compare her stages of development to any other child. All of us develop and grow at different paces and so do four-year-olds.

Provide experiences that will help her explore the world. Take nature walks, go to the zoo, draw on sidewalks (with chalk), and watch the birds. Mother birds are wonderful teachers.

Encourage social occasions with other family adults. We may think they are acting out, but in reality they are misbehaving to get reactions from a new audience.

Abide by the parents' methods of discipline. This can be a great debate, but it is actually a good by-product of being a Grandparent.

You already know this is going to require a great deal of energy. Get plenty of rest when she isn't there and take care of yourself.

Q: I read about several Grandparents that are paid to baby-sit their Grandchildren. I do not get any money for taking care of my Grandson three days a week and have never really expected to be paid. I am now wondering if my Grandson would be better off in a day care with children his own age. I promise this has nothing to do with money.

My other children have never asked me to baby-sit and they do feel that my daughter is taking advantage of me.

What do you think?

Betty, Kingston

Dear Betty,

Baby-sitting Grandchildren is such an individual decision that I never feel we should go by rules or what someone else chooses.

My mother took care of my first son when I began college. I did not have the money to pay for a sitter and she loved her Grandparenting role. After the second son, she decided that she could not take care of two. I understood, cut back on my classes, and hired short-term help.

The questions we should ask:

* What role do I want to play in my Grandchildren's lives? It is valid information that the more you are involved, the closer the relationship will be. But do not feel obligated. This may make you feel more resentment than closeness. How involved do you want your role to be?

* What are your needs? If you have more than one Grandchild, work part or full time, or travel, you have to respect your personal lifestyle. Do you need some extra money that your children are willing to pay?

* What are the needs of others? Many young couples do need help and you want to be of assistance. Baby-sitting may be one

way that will relieve some financial burdens, but helping to pay for some of the Grandchildren's needs would work for many families. How much of yourself can you put into meeting the needs of your adult children?

Gayle Peterson, author of *Making Healthy Families*, says, "Being a happy Grandparent means that there must be a successful fit between your needs and the needs of your adult children in caring for the next generation."

Find the balance that works for your desires and meets the relationship of your family.

Q: My daughter recently moved to Pulaski and has asked me to keep her ten- and twelve-year-old sons after school. Help!!

I haven't been around children in a very long time and I am afraid I won't know what to say to them for three hours every afternoon. Don't misunderstand me; I am anxious to do this.

I have never lived close to them and now have the opportunity. I just don't want to blow it!

Mamma, Pulaski

Dear Mamma,

As long as you really want to do this, you are already started in the right direction. You will have a lot to learn from them, but first you might need to come up with some adult questions.

Start the conversation:

* What TV shows do you watch that remind you of your family? How?

* What are the latest trends in school clothes? Dress codes? Shoes?

* As a Grandmother, I wouldn't want to embarrass you. What would I wear that would make me look dorky? What words are

out of style now? Can you help me become the Grandmother of your dreams?
* Would you ever want to be in the Olympics? Doing What? Why?
* Who is one of your heroes and why?

Things to never do:
* Correct their grammar as soon as it happens. (Work on that another way.)
* Avoid opinion. (If their view differs from yours, allow time to listen to their outlook and then softly explain yours.)
* Talk down to them.
* Pick on insignificant matters (hair styles, clothes they wear, sloppy walking, etc.).
* Be judgmental.
* Criticize.

Ways to pass the time:
* Ask about their hobbies and help them pursue those.
* Read up on topics that might be of interest to them and discuss what you have discovered.
* Take them to the library.
* Ask them to teach you something.

This is going to be a wonderful experience for all of you. Relax, love them, and allow them to be who they are!

———————— READERS RESPOND TO READERS ————————

I wanted to comment on Grandparents baby-sitting. My mother baby-sat for me while I worked. We treated it as a job. She arrived at a certain time in the morning and I was expected to return directly after work. I paid my mother a small payment whenever she baby-sat while I was working (much cheaper than daycare).

This arrangement worked well for everyone. My mother never felt taken advantage of and I was informed of every activity or cute comment from the children.

She would baby-sit at other times (parents night out) just like any Grandparent would do. Another agreement we had was that she not do dishes or clean. She was just to take care of my children.

We moved here from New York two months ago and the boys really miss seeing their Grandparents on a regular basis. Grandma and Grandpa also miss being able to visit. They are glad that they made the decision to baby-sit and were able to be so intimately involved in their care as infants. It was a great arrangement for everyone.

Laurie, Franklin

I am a great-Grandmother and help my daughter take care of her Grandchildren. Her husband is at home a lot and helps to take care of them also. They put their life on hold and devoted themselves to the babies. They are top priority over everything except church, and their deep religious beliefs are why their mother wanted them to be raised as she was raised.

These girls are the luckiest kids in the world to have the Grandparents they have. My daughter's health was not good and she said now she doesn't have time to be sick. I had by-pass surgery and she says the babies gave me a reason to live.

I think my daughter and son-in-law are the greatest Grandparents in the world.

Lela, Old Hickory

Q: I am a great-Grandmother, seventy-two years old. I have agreed to baby-sit with a six- and eight-year-old. I had thought I could take care of them, but I overheard them talking about a friend that was "sniffing glue." I am afraid I am too far behind the times to continue this responsibility.

Can you help me?

Vera, Henderson

Dear Vera,

Believe it or not, most of the baby-sitting being done today is by great-Grandparents. Grandmothers are active with their careers, busy with schedules, and many feel they are due the weekend to relax with their spouse or friends.

You are not too old to take the responsibility if you feel up to the task physically. You can read up on the problems as they confront you. Your years of experience will give you an added dash of expertise in dealing with people of any age. Use your local library to locate information. Take the children with you and study topics jointly.

Check out a book on drugs or household chemicals or handling peer pressure. As you learn together, they will make decisions based on facts. Frances Keppel said, "Education is too important to be left solely to the educators."

Marty Iroff, a local drug expert says, "Glue sniffers can be determined by the smell of glue on their breath. Usually their eyes will be red and watery. Watch for plastic or paper bags, or handkerchiefs containing dried plastic cement. This is a telltale sign that glue-sniffing is being practiced."

If you begin to teach these youngsters early about the hazards of drugs, you will probably save their lives for the future. Learning the facts concerning the effects of drug abuse are the first steps toward a mature behavioral value judgment.

Do not sermonize, for they will immediately stop listening. Most young people appreciate frank talks and may see this as a sign of maturity to reject drugs rather than to abuse them.

Enjoy your summer great-Grandmother! You have a lot to share and they have a lot of joy to give.

Q: *My daughter is to have major surgery next month and I have agreed to help her ten-year-old son.*

We have gotten along well on short visits, but I am not sure how I am expected to treat him for a month. This is not just for overnight!

I am scared of doing something stupid and ruining our relationship forever.

What do ten-year-old boys need? I only raised girls and don't know much about boys.

Marion, Spring Hill

Dear Marion,

We all need to remember that this is the time most young people begin their insecure stage.

A child's self-confidence is easily bruised and it is important for you to provide daily opportunities for him to accomplish small tasks that provide a sense of achievement and self-worth.

Younger children and teenagers are full of self-confidence, but around the age of nine or ten, apprehension about their body and mind begin to take toll on their experiences.

Your Grandson has probably begun to realize he can't do everything, and that is a difficult emotion to deal with. He is beginning to reason things through and recognize consequences of his actions.

They begin to imagine their friends don't like them and common logic will get you nowhere.

Adults have to provide opportunities to feel worthwhile, for children of any age, but particularly this period.

You can find simple projects that you know he will be able to accomplish.

Don't tell on me, but I remember the time we let our Grandson mow the yard for his first time—under close supervision. He didn't do an excellent job, but he did it by himself and was thrilled. He couldn't wait to tell his parents.

Bragging on children in front of others is one of the quickest ways to make a child feel special and needed.

Anything you can do to build their self-esteem is going to pay big dividends later.

This is also the stage when children begin to find a role model to idolize. Provide your Grandson with opportunities to meet older people you would like for him to admire. Make sure the person is worthy of that esteem and possibly will be able to interact with him on a project.

Love him, feed him well (body *and* the psyche), and the two of you will have a Grand time.

Q: *My daughter, son-in-law, and two Grandchildren (ages four and six) will be in town for New Year's Eve. The adults have been invited out for the evening and I have been asked to baby-sit. I don't mind, but would like to make it a special night for them.*

Do you have any suggestions?

Maria, Winchester

Dear Maria,

Mama Williams always told my sons that New Year's Eve was Old Christmas and Grandchildren must stay all night in order for the elves to revisit them again. I remember their excitement being almost as high as it was for December 25.

She had a second stocking with small, inexpensive gifts, allowed them to stay up late, told stories of her childhood Christmases and her Grandparents. Steve and Tod will never forget Old Christmas.

Norma Mower, a member of my Real Life group, relates that her Grandchildren always spent that night with them; she pretended they were adults and they all had a glorious affair. She said her Grandson, Jeff, was responsible for helping make hors d'oeuvres for their party. "Now that he is grown, he still makes the stuffed celery for any holiday occasion and says this is his responsibility."

Goneau Heath, of the group, tells me her Grandchildren expected to sit up all night and watch movies. "They are older now, but when they were young, they knew it was a special night and could stay up as late as their bodies would allow!"

My personal project for New Year's and visiting Grandchildren is to begin a journal of my life. It is difficult enough for us to get around to writing our remembrances down, but teaching New Year's resolutions can be done through watching us carry through on something we have promised them we will do!

I vow this year to co-author a diary with my Grandchildren. I will ask them to give me questions of things they want to know about my younger days. I will make a beginning so that next year we can read about little Barbara Sue and the fascinating occurrences of her childhood.

(Note: I did finish three of those picture/diaries and their parents appreciated them more than the kids—at this point!)

Q: My Grandchildren spend hours in front of their television set. When they come to our house, that is all they want to do, and I think it is very bad for them. What can I do when baby-sitting to avoid the evils of television?

Thelma, Corryton

Dear Thelma,

First of all, we might make a list of the advantages of watching good television. Most children several years ago learned their first alphabet from *Sesame Street*. They are continually learning geography on our news reports. Biography and the History Channel are wonderful ways to teach. My Grandchildren know more about our earth's atmosphere from the Weather Channel than I am capable of discussing.

Classical movies, such as *Black Beauty, Cinderella,* and *Charlotte's Web* often inspire them to read books by the same author.

So, the real problem isn't watching television, but a matter of proper supervision.

At your house, you might want to substitute this time by doing fun things. You can read to them, take a hike, map out a treasure hunt, plan a scavenger search, cut out paper dolls, make new toys with clay, start a scrapbook, or even learn a new hobby together.

Baby-sitting is so different from years ago. They have been born into a world of technology that occupies most of their waking hours. They are rarely being taught to create or play on their own.

I recently heard a Grandmother who had just spent all day baby-sitting a four-year-old say, "I had been so down on television, until I found this was the easiest way for me to get some peace and quiet. She has no clue how to play by herself."

It is very easy for us to be judgmental about what our Grandchildren should be seeing, but when it comes down to the bottom line, we can only make changes at our house.

Q: I have been so concerned about my Grandchildren this summer. I am almost glad school is starting, but even that scares me. They watch TV all day and play video games that are violent and scary to me.

Is there anything I can do or say that will stop this shocking habit?

Charlotte, Nashville

Dear Charlotte,

You don't mention ages. That makes some difference, but I am like you with the inappropriate material that is so readily available to young people.

I went to the movies several months ago that was R-comedy, but it had won several awards. I won't mention the name because I certainly don't recommend it to anyone. A couple in their seventies was sitting behind me, and we commented on how movies are not what they once were. Most of us remember when Rhett Butler uttered that controversial word—"Damn." What a shocker to us!

The language in this movie was appalling. The sexual content was so explicit and graphic, we could have easily been watching a formerly rated X movie.

The kicker to all of this—two different couples had a total of five children there under the age of ten. One was about five years old. *What on earth were they thinking?*

So that is the question: What are parents and Grandparents considering when they allow this in their homes? Do they think it will not affect their children because they go to church on Sunday, have a professional job, or build our bridges?

I was so proud of my youngest son who refused to have a TV in their home until their daughter was in school. They scrutinized and controlled the movies she saw and the programs she watched, and today she has a good sense about life.

What are we to do? Role model in our own homes, teach the joy of reading good books, and ask questions. Sometimes they want to talk about what they see and hear. Be prepared for a shock on how much they know!

Q: *I read so much about Grandparents that have difficulty disciplining their Grandchildren. I keep my four-year-old Granddaughter four days a week. I am responsible for her behavior and this requires me to have some type of effective discipline.*

I tried time-out periods where I made her sit in a tiny rocker for five minutes. She would get so agitated that I felt I needed to redefine time-out.

"Physical Time-Out" is what I call my new correction system. Although she needs to see this as a form of punishment, it can be a time of learning as well. Sometimes we walk around the backyard, sometimes we go as far as around the block, and all the time I am asking questions about what she is seeing in her surroundings.

She is assigned work that is required if she doesn't behave—work that a four-year-old can learn for later skills. She must stop playing with toys and do Nana's work. I have taught her how to match socks, fold dishcloths, dust my books, and stack magazines.

After she has done these things, I make a list on a board of all the things she has learned to do successfully. Even though she is being punished (or I actually see it as redirecting her unacceptable behavior), she is always so excited to share with her mother what she has learned that day.

Some people may see this in different lights, but with an active child, there are many ways to discipline and teach at the same time. Quiet children may need to be taught in other ways.

Nana, e-mail

Dear Nana,

It is too bad all Grandparents do not see their baby-sitting as a marvelous training ground as effective as you. Even quiet children should learn to match socks!

We do need to remember that time-out of any kind is for the purpose of allowing children to get their disruptive behavior under control. Consistency in discipline is the most important component and should teach children that you will continue to have the same rules, day after day!

Your program sounds very productive as you use your Granddaughter's energy to work for her.

Q: I have just spent a week with my Grandchildren and discovered a very strange activity on their part. Part of my purpose was to enable the parents to go on a business trip while I kept the children in school.

The first night after baths, homework, and talk, I left them to get ready for bed. When I came back thirty minutes later, they were both in bed with their clothes on! I asked, "What on earth is going on?"

"We always get dressed for school before we go to bed," they both explained. "If we don't, we can't get ready on time in the morning."

I quizzed them about their mother knowing and they said she encouraged this behavior.

Am I crazy or what? Have you ever heard of this?

Anonymous

Dear Anonymous,

After reading your letter, I asked around. Much to my surprise also, this does happen.

My friend Norma remembered finding her daughter dressed for high school one night for the same reason—thirty years ago. She made her undress.

Several Grandmothers said they knew their Grandchildren did this occasionally, and some mothers confessed that it sure did save time in the morning for sleepy-headed students.

This goes back to the hectic pace our young people are leading today. When my boys were growing up, they had to be in bed by 8:30 and were able to get up in plenty of time to dress, eat, and get to the bus.

Today's generation has probably been out late at a ballgame, recital, club meeting, or extra tutoring sessions. Our secretary

takes her child to school at 6:30 A.M. in order for him to partici-
pate in a computer class. I would probably sleep with my clothes
on also!

Wonder if the girls put their make-up on at bedtime? No, on
second thought they are doing that while driving. I also wonder when
they find time to put rings in all those extra holes . . .

I am very concerned about the educational structure of our
schools today and the demands that come as young as elementary
school for career choices. What happened to the ones who want to
dream, look out windows, and enjoy their childhood?

Q: *While baby-sitting for a week in Nashville, I read your column about the
houseguests who did appalling things to their hostess. I found myself wanting to
tell you about my visit here.*

*I agreed to baby-sit a week with four active teenagers. I was told by my son
that while they were in Washington, they would need someone here to play taxi
for their various activities. I felt I would enjoy the time with them, and I needed
a break from my own life's hectic schedule.*

*They have maid service and a gardener, so I brought plenty to read. When I
arrived, I found a list of chores my daughter-in-law had prepared for me. Each
day was scheduled. Monday: change the sheets on all the beds (including hers),
wash the sheets, and press the pillowcases. Tuesday: "be sure the house is
completely picked up for the maid and leave nothing on the kitchen counters!"
Wednesday: sort the recyclable materials and take the containers to the end of
their long driveway!*

*The list went on and on. I was so tired by the time I went to soccer, piano lessons,
and tutoring, I felt as if I had been gone a month. I couldn't wait to get home and rest!*

*Yes, I will do it again if I am needed, but the next time I will be the one making
the list of things I will not do!*

Just a Tired Grandmother, Louisville, Kentucky

Dear Grandmother,

You remained calm in the face of an imposing daughter-in-law. I
wonder if your son knew you were asked to do all those chores. But

being the lady you obviously are, you probably didn't tell him. Maybe somebody will read this and not burden their own baby-sitter.

As I get older and wiser, I find personalities of our in-laws dictate much of our actions and verbal comments.

Q: I just read your column about the Grandmother from Louisville, Kentucky, who did a lot of housework while baby-sitting with her Grandchildren in Nashville. I read your column often and usually get lots of helpful hints. This time, however, I can't believe you didn't encourage "kid power."

She said there were four active teenagers—they could have taken care of the recyclables, cleared off the counters, and picked up for the maid.

One summer I had the best time with my Grandkids when we did all the chores jointly and then played together in a clean house. The older boys even enjoyed cooking some of the meals and cleaning up afterwards.

As for changing the sheets and pressing the pillow cases, I could have skipped that job completely. I've discovered the world doesn't end if the sheets aren't changed weekly.

Last Thanksgiving, my Nashville daughter brought dinner from a caterer. She served it, cleaned up, left us a plate for the microwave, and took the leftovers home. Today, in the mail I should get a menu to choose for this year's feast. I can hardly wait.

Shirley, Estell Springs

Dear Shirley,

I hope this Thanksgiving message gets to all daughters and daughters-in-law. What a wonderful present for the holidays. You've done a miraculous job of training your daughter.

You are right! I dropped the ball and should have suggested that the Grandmother enlist the aid of the children to keep the house in top shape. This is one of the areas I feel some of our young parents are failing—not preparing their children for the real world.

My boys learned how to wash, cook, and make their own beds. I did not work during those years and had the time, but felt that was part of my job in parenting. My daughters-in-law are very thankful today!

Responsibility is a value that seems to have gone out with manners and decorum. Piano lessons, soccer, and computer games have become higher priorities.

Q: My daughter will not let me baby-sit because I have told her I will spank her children if they misbehave.

How else does she think I am going to make them mind? I am not going to allow them to run wild or do things that might hurt them.

Do you spank your Grandchildren?

Nora, Goodlettsville

Dear Nora,

I don't remember ever spanking any of my Grandchildren. You might need to ask them.

Sean tells me he remembers a time I did get mad. "You looked *so* mean that day!" I have tried to never look mean again!

My daddy never spanked me, although his discussion of the crime was often worse than any whipping. He could make me feel *so* guilty. My mother spanked!

Dr. Rachel Thomas, a leading authority on child development says, "Spanking is not effective. Time-Out is the best way to teach a child his behavior is inappropriate.

"He should be delegated to a dull, non-stimulating place and remain there for a predetermined amount of time. Young children (between two to five years of age) need only five minutes. The length of time is not as important as the message that you are in control."

In a previous column, a Grandmother talked about how she required work instead of Time-Out. You might want to think of a more flexible method of discipline.

I have always felt that a discussion about the error is a good way to begin. The second method is to take away something that is very meaningful—for a short time.

Maybe your daughter feels you are too eager to spank. It sounds as if you are anticipating trouble and that is almost a disaster prophesied.

Maybe you need to be thinking more of what you can be doing to entertain your Grandchildren.

If you can change your attitude, talk to your daughter again.

Q: *Our three-year-old Grandson always cries when he stays all night with us.*

He says he is afraid of the dark, but his parents tell us this never happens at home. Are we doing something wrong? How can we make him more comfortable at our house?

Vanessa, Murfreesboro

Dear Vanessa,

When our Grandson, Tyler, was two years old, he developed a fear of the dark. I thought his mother was very original, when she made him a "Monster Gun."

She took a spray bottle, covered it with brightly colored paper, and filled it with purple water. When he went to bed at night, he took his "gun," and when he thought he saw the monster in his room, he "sprayed" them away! It worked!

Your Grandson is staying in a strange bed and sleeping away from his parents. No matter how much he loves you in the daytime, the dark offers new and scary times for a three-year-old.

Try the monster gun!

Q: *My divorced daughter works a split shift, and I keep her children most of the time.*

It is easy for you to say, "Just love them," but I feel like I should be instilling some kind of guidance with their lives.

What is the most important training you think I should be concentrating on?

Judy, Donelson

Dear Judy,

I do admit that Grandparenting is very different when you are doing a large part of the rearing.

All of my Grandchildren are fortunate enough to have full-time parents that are doing an excellent task of preparing them for adulthood.

Dr. Theodore Isaac Rubin, child psychiatrist, says, "Paramount to building a child is to develop their self-esteem, confidence, and independence."

All of that sounds overwhelming to think of at one time, but if you begin to cultivate the self-esteem portion of this philosophy, the rest will follow. All of the books available today on self-esteem did not exist when most of us were attempting to direct the lives of our young people.

Self-esteem is how you actually feel about yourself—not what your outward personality indicates. It is important to teach young children how to feel good about themselves. Remember youngsters read your thoughts and feelings much more clearly than they listen to what you are saying, so you must believe in their abilities and their potential.

Find out what they like to do and develop that ambition. Look at their talents and encourage their abilities. The most important ingredient, according to my Grandparenting group, is accepting each unique human being for their individual potential and not trying to make them into someone else.

It is hard enough to find out "who you are" at any age, but it surely complicates the personality if an adult it trying to turn you into someone else.

Q: *My daughter is having her first child and she lives in the same town with us. She has started hinting about me taking care of the baby so she can go back to work. I have other Grandchildren who live out of town, and I have taken care of them for their parents to go on trips, but I don't want the full responsibility of baby-sitting all the time.*

We have had a good relationship most of her life and I don't want this to change anything. How do I decline without hurting her feelings? I do have a busy life and had not planned to give up any of my own plans.

I don't want to sound heartless, but I have heard of so many Grandparents complain about all the baby-sitting they do, that I don't want to become resentful.

How do other Grandparents tell their children "no"?

B. E., Shelbyville

Dear B. E.,

The readers are first going to be concerned that you are unable to say "no" to your daughter.

You need to remember that you are in control of your life. Having Grandchildren can be a wonderful thing, but the choice to have them is the responsibility of your daughter.

Explain that you just can't take on this tremendous responsibility at this time, but that you will be willing to pinch-hit in an emergency.

A friend of mine was also approached with this dilemma. She agreed to take the baby two days a week. The other Grandmother took two days, and Aunt Beth took the remaining day. I think this must be confusing, but it works for them.

Baby-sitting can cause tension in families and you can always be supportive of your daughter in other ways.

Now, the other sort of Grandparent is going to tell you that this is the most awesome experience of their lives. "Taking care of my Grandchildren is much easier and lots more fun than raising children. I wouldn't have missed this for the world," says Bethel Smith. She has taken care of three Grandchildren for their mothers to be able to work full time.

A Grandparent's individual personality dictates which direction you go, but don't feel guilty whatever you decide.

-------------------- READERS RESPOND TO READERS --------------------

These comments from several Grandparents help us to realize there is no right or wrong way, just a right time!

GRANDPARENTS' CORNER

I keep reading all these letters from people who are so thrilled with baby-sitting their Grandchildren full time. What is wrong with them?

Why would they want to get saddled with raising their children's kids? I raised mine and have no intentions of starting all over again.

Sarah, Columbia

I have spent a lot of years taking care of my children and working to make sure that my retirement years are the very best they can be. I don't feel it is my responsibility be take care of my Grandchildren—even thought I love them as if they were my own.

Retired in Franklin

Taking care of my Grandchildren would probably be worthwhile and advantageous to everyone, but I just don't feel physically capable of keeping up with their energy. I am not in "poor health." I walk two miles every day, take my vitamins, and travel every chance I get. I am involved with clubs, church, and friends, but taking care of children is a different kind of stress and activity.

We should not be made to feel guilty that we aren't baby-sitting our Grandchildren all the time.

Happy Granny, Lafayette

Q: After reading some comments like:"Grandparenting is not always so Grand," I find days when I'm not in a "Nana" mood either, but I try to work around that by contacting my Grandchildren at least weekly. I can find out then if they are in a "Nana" mood. Sometimes they want to spend a weekend, sometimes not. You have to be flexible and try not to get your feelings hurt by rejections.

I have a thirteen-year-old Granddaughter. I enjoy her so much. We have lots in common, but I try not to focus on her, for I am an Equal Opportunity Nana. My fifteen-year-old Grandson is quiet, but we still manage to stay on the same wavelength. He knows he can talk to me about anything—and I mean anything!

What I am trying to say is: Don't think you have to be an old-fashioned Grandparent. Work, play, and spend quality time with your Grandchildren, even if it is over the phone. I send lots of silly cards and cartoons to my Grandchildren.
Sandy, Nashville

Dear Equal Opportunity Nana,

I love your title!

Several have written to tell me ways in which they are able to enjoy their time with their Grandchildren. Aretha wrote to say, "When I am not eager to baby-sit, I just give my children an IOU for a later time. So far, this has worked with them and no one came away upset." I am going to be trying this!

Marion from Columbia wrote to say that she sets herself a maximum of hours she will gladly baby-sit in a month and her children keep up with it and know never to go over that limit. Sometimes, they don't use it all up, but "they can't carry it over to another month. This way I feel I am in control of the situation."

A reader from Lebanon wrote to say, "I feel I am overworked as a baby-sitter and sometimes don't like any of my family!"

MONEY

Q: I have two Grandchildren who live near me. They are ten- and twelve-year-old boys. They are always asking for money. I have never given them much at a time, but now they are older and I do have to hire someone to help me get some of my work done. Do you think it is OK to pay them to help me?
Employer Granny, Cookeville

Dear Granny,

I vote yes! What a wonderful way to help with their spending money, while you are being assisted with your chores. But, you must ask their parents how they feel about it and what they think you should pay them. What could seem reasonable to you might insult the children or what tremendous amount you might want to give them could damage their earning expectations forever!

Make a list of the work you want done and relate the money amount to be given when they have completed the work.

Painting fences, cleaning garages, weeding flower beds, moving boxes from attics or storage are all tasks that can be done by children, while training them to be good employees.

Once they are old enough to drive, running errands and shopping for you is an ideal way to teach adult expectations of life.

Mary Elizabeth Garner tells me she often planned for her friends to come for lunch and hired her sixteen-year-old Granddaughter to cater and serve. Mary was capable of doing all this, but it gave the Granddaughter a job and made Mary's friends feel special.

Robert Bailey gave his riding mower to his Grandson to use for a summer job. The only payment required was to mow Robert's yard every ten days.

One of my mother's favorite stories was about a ten-year-old neighbor that had asked to dust my furniture for some spending money. She unexpectedly answered my phone with, "This is the maid speaking!" My embarrassment was eased by hearing how thrilled she was to have a pretend job.

I admit most of today's ten-year-old girls would not want to be a maid, but you can be creative with a job title.

Q: We have Grandchildren away at college and don't know of any new ways to remind them we love them.

Don't suggest money or food. We are out of both.

Grandmother of Eight in College, Smyrna

Dear Grandmother of Eight,

Well, have you tried:

* Writing a message on a balloon and slipping the deflated surprise in your next letter? Any age gets a kick out of balloons.

* Next time you go out to eat, ask for the menu and describe the details of your night out on the classy stationery.

* Write a mystery letter with invisible ink, including instructions on how to make your words appear.

* Find a picture of your Grandchild's parent as a child and tell an unusual story about them at that age. Maybe even the details of when and why the photograph was snapped.

* Pretend you are a child and write a note asking them for money. It will be interesting to see how they react to a reversal of roles. It is fun to be creative and college students can get the joke. High school students would not be impressed with these corny messages.

Q: My daughter-in-law says I spoil my Grandchildren and she doesn't like for them to come over to our house.

What can I do? Is there anything I could say to her? Aren't Grandparents allowed to spoil their Grandchildren some?

Alice, Oliver Springs

Dear Alice,

Grandparents are distinctive in that we are able to spend time with our Grandchildren and then withdraw from the picture when we get tired or we have simply had enough.

We are usually able to spend more quality time and money on them than we did our children. We often feel we have earned the right to do this. We love the attention we receive from our Grandchildren and most of them love every minute of our fun times with them.

Consequently, we are labeled "spoilers." It is difficult for parents to work at being the enforcer of rules and promoter of values every day and yet watch their children dash into a Grandparent's arms and receive only joyful words.

You need to remember how it was when you were the parent, not the Grandparent. Your daughter-in-law needs to recognize that

Grandparents are for a special purpose in their children's lives—Mutual Admiration Society.

Sit down and talk to her about your different roles and assure her that you will do nothing to contradict her discipline and control.

Q: *Every time I give my Grandson money, he spends it on such foolish things.*

Should I stop giving him money and take a chance on giving him a gift he doesn't want?

John, Pulaski

Dear John,

What may be foolish to you may not be foolish to a child.

Don't give money with strings attached. When Grandparents give money, we should be giving because we want the Grandchild to select something he or she wants—not necessarily what we want him or her to have.

Q: *I may be way off base with this problem, but I am eager to hear your opinion. As our Grandchildren got older, we began to give them money for their birthday. After all, how do you know how to choose clothes or tapes for kids?*

Last month, our ten-year-old Granddaughter shyly asked, "What are you going to get me for my birthday?" Her birthday had been three weeks before and I knew we had sent a card with money enclosed.

I asked her mother about it and she didn't remember the card coming. I asked the child to go search through her cards and she found it.

Her mother said, "Oh yes, I put the money in her college fund!" The child wailed about that not being fair. I felt the same.

What about you?

Put-Out Granny, Knoxville

Dear Put-Out,

In order to keep up with what the younger generation is thinking, I checked with some of my friends who have pre-teens.

Laura, Janice, and Carolyn all agreed that this was not fair to the child. If she were older and more aware of what a college fund was going to mean, it would make a difference.

Martha Ann said, "Even if the Granddaughter is mature and wants this to be done, the Grandparents should have been told about the decision beforehand."

LeaAnn suggested some Grandparents might want to help toward a fund, but do it on another occasion. "Birthdays are for fun things!"

We give money to our older Grandchildren and their thank-you notes usually explain, "I spent the money on . . ." This indicates the children's decision to spend the money on something they wanted.

Next time I would give a gift certificate or take the Granddaughter shopping when you are together. Mother means well. She is thinking of the future. You and I are enjoying one day at a time.

Q: I had a problem with my daughter-in-law about buying clothes for my new Granddaughter.

She said, "I know what she needs, and you don't need to buy anything for her."

I had already bought several things when she was born and had noticed she had never let her wear them. This really hurt my feelings. I finally talked to my son about it and, naturally, he defended his wife's decision, but added: "I want you to take the money you were going to spend on Alisha and spend it on yourself."

I have taken him at his word and whenever I see a cute little outfit I am tempted to buy, I just note the price and spend the same amount on something unnecessary for myself. I have other Grandchildren and I continue to be able to buy for them as I want.

I do have a problem with being late on birthdays and this sure does miff aforementioned daughter-in-law. Any ideas from your group on this?

Dorris, Lebanon

Dear Dorris,

Thanks for the tip on unwanted presents. I am sure lots of Grandparents face this problem for one reason or another.

Forgetfulness! Yes, what do we do about this problem? One friend said that she keeps a large calendar in her kitchen. Every morning when she gets up, she checks to see what day it is and marks it off and says, "Well, I lived to see another one—Hallelujah!"

She went on to add that she copies all the birthdays for a year on her new calendars and that way she never forgets.

Daryl sits down once a month and addresses cards for the entire month. He puts the date he wants to mail them in the corner for the stamp and keeps them where he sees them every day. When the particular date rolls up, he stamps and sends them on their way—feeling relieved and confident.

If a gift is to be included, he attaches a note, so he will get it bought and wrapped on time.

One of my daughters-in-law had taught me to buy cards by the box, because they are much more economical. Today, most of the females in our family are stamping and making our own cards. We may not really be saving money, but we sure are having fun together.

Remember, we are allowed to forget where we left our glasses, or where we put our savings account book, or why we bought that ghastly dress, or who sang at our son's wedding, or why we went into the kitchen, but we are *never* allowed to forget birthdays.

Q: Christmas shopping has really become a chore, especially for my younger Grandchildren. Can you make any suggestions?

Brian, Nashville

Dear Brian,

One of the greatest gifts we can give a child is instilling a love for books.

Jim Trelease, author of *The New Read-Aloud Handbook*, was in Knoxville recently. He had just become a Grandparent and was especially aware of his new obligations. He suggested that we select a book and then read the story to a tape recorder. A memorable tape and book makes for a very special Christmas present.

For little ones, choose a picture book that will be easy for them to follow your delightful voice. You might even make personal comments or tell them when to turn the page.

Most of the Dr. Seuss and Shel Silverstein books are wonderful for reading aloud to little ones. The pictures are so much fun and your pronunciation of the nonsensical words and rhymes will thrill any Grandchild.

As your Grandchildren get older, remember that most children listen three to five grades above their reading ability. If they aren't ready to read "chapter books" yet, this might be the time to introduce them. They can listen as long as their mind is interested. You can tape in short sessions, letting your voice and enthusiasm rest in between.

You might buy them a good bed lamp so they can read to themselves at night. Our boys were allowed to leave their light on as long as they were reading. I notice they both have the same rule for their children.

Q: Christmas shopping for Grandchildren is getting more difficult and expensive every year. They seem to have so much and yet there are so many things that are being advertised on television. Can you help me know where to start?

Faye, Concord

Dear Faye,

Most of us did not get an overabundance of expensive gifts when we were growing up. We remember the specialness of the day for reasons other than gifts. The mystic wonder, the lengthy suspense, the spicy smells, the family togetherness—these are memories that made up our holidays.

Grandparents' gifts often get lost in the array of other "more exciting" presents, so the Real Life group suggests you might want to do yours early or later.

Hazel Whitehead pieced a quilt and let her Granddaughter select the colors and arrange the squares. She would sit on the unfinished quilt and ask, "How soon will it be until Christmas, so I can take it to my house?"

Betty Tobin knitted afghans for her Grandchildren from the yarn of old sweaters, caps, and socks their parents had worn.

Lavonda Teboe made coupon books for her Grandchildren consisting of shopping trips, meals out, and movies. They get to decide when to "cash" them in.

Norma Mower is making her Granddaughter a cookbook from recipes clipped from the paper and magazines, along with lessons in cooking and tips for cleaning.

I bought my Granddaughter a copy of my favorite book at her age, *Heidi*.

Be original. They need memories from you, not another toy to be broken and discarded by January first.

Q: I read your column about giving gifts to Grandchildren. One of our Granddaughters (now nineteen years and away in college) wrote to ask if she was too old to continue our Christmas lunch tradition.

When she was only two, I felt that my Christmas gift would be lost in the shuffle and flurry of all the other presents and I didn't want that. Not that my gift was anything special, but I simply wanted her to remember what I had given her.

I decided to take her to lunch at a special restaurant. At that time two was awfully young to be going fancy, but we did anyway! Maybe it was the surroundings, or the Sunday dress she had on, but she behaved beautifully. We ate lunch, opened her present, and had a great outing.

We have done that every year since. Is she too old? Never—as long as she wants to do that with her Memaw.

Marion, Nashville

Q: My Granddaughter suggested I write to tell you about our Christmas tradition. When she was little, I started a necklace for her with a tiny gold nugget, made from an old ring of mine. Every year, my husband and I add another nugget or a pearl.

Her necklace is very unique and lovely. She looks forward to seeing what will be added each Christmas.

Lucille, Columbia

Dear Marion and Lucille,

What very lucky Grandchildren. I think Grandparents' traditions should be an expression we are teaching about ourselves. Sometimes we often mistake lots of stuff as a sign of love.

Q: I have two sons and one of them has been financially successful. His children want for nothing. My younger son has never been able to keep a job very long and I have had to help his children with their basic needs.

I am thinking of writing a new will. Do I divide my money equally or do I leave the bulk to the children of the one who has no money?

V. C., Westmoreland

Dear V. C.,

Wow, this really divided the Real Life group. Ralph emphatically declared, "Divide it equally; it is the only fair way."

Ted said, "No, the other has needs and can maybe provide a better education with more money."

The entire group was concerned with the "whys" the younger son couldn't keep a job. Would he be able to manage a significant amount of money if you gave it to him for his children?

Several wanted you to spend your money now on the younger son's children. Hazel commented, "Just remember it is your money and you should do with it what makes you feel good. There is no right or wrong answer."

They all feel you should consult an estate planner and see what would be the best option for your Grandchildren's future.

Another important consideration—money isn't everything; you shouldn't just dwell on your financial gifts. Loving memories of time well spent will reap more rewards for them than any amount of money you may leave.

Q: *Two of my Grandchildren have wealthy Grandparents. They are always giving them money. My income is limited. How can I compete with this?*

Shirley, Nashville

Dear Shirley,

Are you trying to buy them or love them?

In all my research with young people, I always ask, "What are Grandparents for?" Money is not even in the top five of their answers, but "*love me*" is number one. That doesn't cost anything and lasting memories are usually created by adoration and kindness. Be thankful the other Grandparents have finances available. It will mean a great deal for your Grandchildren's educational opportunities!

Q: *I have a money problem with my older son. I do not get to see their children. He and his wife have been married thirty-four years and have indoctrinated their daughters against me. They won't even speak. My son will call me on the phone occasionally, but he is hostile.*

I am seventy-nine years old. When his father passed away, he asked for his inheritance! I gave him a nice gift of money, but he said it wasn't a "drop in the bucket" for the amount that he deserved. I gave my younger son the same and he was very happy.

I have written my will and only left the older son a pittance. My younger son says not to worry, that he will take care of me. I have an excellent relationship with his family. I love my older son, but his wife and children will have nothing to do with us.

Please ask your Real Life group what they think I should do.

Depressed in Gallatin

Dear Depressed,

They want to know where he got the idea that he "deserved" any of your money?

Our local paper recently ran a story about a couple that had worked hard and invested well. They had no children. He died several years ago. She died last month. She left their money to people who had been kind to them. Their college-age yard boy received 10 percent, their veterinarian 10 percent, their next door neighbor 10 percent, etc.

Everyone was surprised at the will. "I didn't know they had money," the yard boy declared, "I was nice because they were always kind to me."

Your money should go to people who are sincerely "kind" to you!

The Real Life group says to do what is comfortable for you; however they are not fans of children who forsake their parents in later years.

Chapter 5

MORALITY OR COMMON SENSE

Pierced Noses, Where You Sleep,
and Humanity

THANK-YOU NOTES WERE THE TOPIC OF TOO MANY letters. If I had asked Grandparents to list their number one pet peeve, I am convinced 99 percent of them would say, "lack of thank-you cards."

As Dr. Laura might callously remark, "I am here to blame the parents and then their parents." Where do you fall in this genealogy trail?

You will probably say you made your children write thank-you notes, but how did you go about it?

I have an obsessive friend who typed all of her son's graduation thank-you cards and "forced" him to actually take the time to sit down and sign them! What did he learn? Zilch!

How many of you "nagged" your children until they wrote those notes? How many of you played the guilt trip on them? How many said, "Oh, let's just call and that will be sufficient"?

As a former teacher, I believe in the old adage that if we teach a child to enjoy learning—it will stick. Adults who do not like to read never learn to love the written word. Those who never write thank-you notes will miss out on appreciating the thrill of expressing their thoughts.

How much skill does it take? Very little. A smidgen of sincerity, a pen, paper, and a stamp. Oh, yes, time. That is the killer.

"I am too busy to sit down and write." How many hours are you spending watching ball games? How many hours on the computer? How much time on the telephone?

Setting an example is my number two method of teaching. I still find myself doing things my mother did, just because I assume I am supposed to do it. There may have been periods in my life when I didn't want to be like her, although she taught me lessons that I will never forget.

Now that we have solved the major problem—let's move on to more interesting subjects. Here again, we find a totally different set of questions than my Grandparents were asking.

Q: I have been reading much about the controversy over whether children should or should not be sleeping with their parents. Our Grandchildren have always slept in our bed when they come to visit. Now, I am beginning to worry about this habit. What do you think?

Sarah, Nashville

Dear Sarah,

This is one of those splendid times that being a Grandparent gives you a "different" rule. Parents—NO! Grandparents—MAYBE!

Children who sleep with their parents are not learning independence. If they are scared at night, a soothing bedtime story in their own bed will usually settle their minds. Parents also need the privacy of their own room. What other time is most available for sharing secrets and love?

Our Grandchildren's habit of snoozing in a sleeping bag in our bedroom started many years ago, and each one has felt it a benefit and thrill of being at our house.

A few years ago, the two girls (then six and eight) both started on the floor, but by morning they were both in our bed, along with the dog. The image of that scene will tell you why we amended the rules on "crowded" nights.

Differences in family traditions will set the rules for individual cases. Family atmosphere will determine who sleeps where, but in ideal situations I see no reason for Grandchildren occasionally sharing sleeping quarters.

My son called last week to tell me how good their new guest bed slept. "Why were you sleeping there?" his inquisitive mother asked. "Jessie offered half of her allowance to sleep with us just one night and you know how she kicks. I moved!" Oh well, there are exceptions to every rule!

I wasn't allowed to sleep with my own Grandparents—even had to sleep upstairs, alone and frightened! The memory is somewhat softened by the remembrance of a bottomless feather-bed. The vision remains of being in heaven on a cloud, buried weightless in puffs of fuzz and warmth.

That is an experience our Grandchildren have missed and will only be able to imagine in their fantasies. Maybe we try to revise the scene with united coziness. Grandchildren need all the secure and comfortable love they can manage. Our goal of becoming a refuse in time of stress should begin early in order to carry them through the traumatic teens and adolescent adulthood.

Q: We are having a problem that concerns our nine-year-old Granddaughter. She and her mother visit often. We began noticing little things missing some time ago. Recently the TV remote was not in the room, but turned up on another visit in a pillow case. The next time she was here, there were three cut glass prisms missing from an antique lighting fixture. Another time, some antique marbles and a gold-plated ladies' pen.

What we do not understand is how she keeps these hidden from her family. She has an older brother who is sixteen years old. She is our only daughter's child, and we don't want to tell her she is a thief.

On the other hand, we do not like the idea of her growing up with these kinds of values. Would you please help us to do what is right about her?

Someone Distressed in Middle Tennessee

Dear Distressed Grandmother,

When I was your Granddaughter's age, my Grandfather lived in the country and had a big mailbox by the side of the road. One day, I stuffed it full of leaves and trash. I thought it would be funny for the mailman to find.

A couple of days later, my Grandfather casually told me about this terrible thing that had happened to him. It seems that someone put trash in his mailbox and since that was federal property, he had to pay a large fine. It was my lesson about vandalism.

I would try the "someone stole . . . and we think it might have been . . ." This could be someone she knows—a cleaning lady, friend across the street, etc. I would go into the consequences of stealing, possible charges, and how other people look at thieves.

She may be telling them you gave her those pieces. You might ask her mother if she has seen any of your antique marbles, etc. "They may have fallen in your luggage on a visit."

If none of these do any good, you are going to have to talk to your daughter. If this is happening in other places, the consequences may not be as pleasant.

Q: Today's society's complete disregard for values has me upset! I feel like no one is trying to teach ethics or morals. White-collar criminals, hypocritical church members, and millionaire entertainers are no example to set before young people.

Mothers are working outside the home and leaving their children for us Grandparents to raise. How do we combat what they see and hear from the rest of the world?

Discouraged in Crossville, Tennessee

Dear Discouraged,

Aletha Brodine, a Real Life member, tells the story of a young neighbor child who would "borrow" items from her—never to return them. "I decided if no one else was going to teach her the meaning of the word, I should!"

Aletha "borrowed" the offender's favorite necklace, didn't return it, and waited. The youngster soon came to ask for it back. After Aletha's inquiry as to the meaning of the word, the child understood she had not been "borrowing."

We can give all the sage advice in the world, but only sporadically will anyone listen. The ideal way to show young people the acceptable behavior is to be a role model with values.

"Values like honor (honesty and integrity in one's actions), respect (sense of worth for oneself and others), and conscience (right or wrong conduct and motive) are traits to be displayed as a badge," states Dr. Martin Crews, psychologist and Grandfather of six. "The secret is wearing your badge without having to spell it out."

How do we teach good ethics if we lie about the child's age to get a cheaper ticket to an activity, take a handful of grapes at the grocery store as we shop, blame others for our own mistakes, gossip maliciously about our neighbors, or show disrespect to employees in restaurants or department stores? We could all make a list of pervasive sins.

We should all be teaching values through our behavior. I hope my Grandchildren see genuine kindness, considerate manners, and an active conscience that is willing to apologize when my mouth or actions betray my dark side.

There is a lot of discouraging conduct in our world today, but there is always hope. To reword the song, "Let there be values on earth and let them begin with me" should be the endeavor of those who think the world is going to h——— in a hand basket.

Q: This is a concern that has probably been discussed many times, but I can't find anybody that agrees on the solution.

Our three-year-old Grandson is still sucking his thumb. He sucks it all the time. If he were an adult, he would be called a chain smoker!

His parents still think it is cute, but I worry about his teeth. He is small for his age and, so far, no one has commented on this baby habit.

Do you have any suggestions for me to give the parents?

Granny Eli, Clarksville

Dear Granny Eli,

My first suggestion is *not* to make suggestions unless the advice is solicited.

Meme Stephens thinks thumb sucking is a normal reflex for babies. It relaxes and comforts them. Usually children quit between two and three years of age, but adulthood is supposed to come at eighteen. How many eighteen-year-old teenagers do you feel are mature and ready for the real world? Children progress at their own individual pace.

Some children tend to suck their thumbs because they are feeling insecure, brought about by changes in their little world. A new baby, a new house, a new sitter, etc. Focus on helping the child feel comfortable with whatever is going on around him.

A pediatric dentist told me that this dental problem could begin about age four. Their pediatrician will bring up the issue when he feels there is a problem.

Maybe I am very sympathetic because I was a thumb sucker. I obviously went beyond the four year cut-off because I remember distinctly Mother putting some foul tasting medicine on my thumbs. I endured the taste long enough to dissolve it and then resumed my "baby habit."

It seems strange that I can't recall where I hide my "mad money," but I can pleasantly awaken those memories of several decades ago. This may prove the adage—we remember what we want to.

If anyone should ask, you might suggest putting socks on the little ones hands at night and brightly-colored bandages on those thumbs during the day.

Q: *My daughter is having a difficult time getting her son to give up his pacifier. They are leaving him with us for a week, and I was hoping you had heard of some new methods.*

Mary, Knoxville

Dear Mary,

Great! I have been waiting nearly a year to relate this incident. While shopping in Toys R Us, I saw an energetic mother and her young "pacifier sucking" daughter looking at Barbie dolls. The mother kept asking, "Are you sure you want to do this?"

"Umhuh," mumbled the little one. Consequently in the checkout line, ahead of me, was the same pair. The mother placed the chosen Barbie on the counter and told the cashier, "Melissa has a trade-in for the doll."

Melissa took one last, lingering draw and abandoned the pacifier on the counter. "I trade you Passy for Barbie," she whispered.

The perceptive cashier smiled and said, "Fine, do you want Barbie wrapped or would you rather carry her?"

As Melissa adjusted Barbie's jumpsuit, the young mother paid for the doll and nodded "yes" to trashing the "Passy."

I rushed to walk out with the mother. "Do you think this will work?"

"A couple of friends tried it with their children and their Passy was never mentioned again. It seems to signify a maturing process in their minds," she related.

So, if the "dog ate it" or dipping it in broccoli hasn't worked, you might want to teach the art of trade to your Grandson.

Q: I have two Granddaughters, ages two and four, who do not get along. They are cousins. The two-year-old is always attacking her older cousin—pulling hair, biting, and so on. She is the only person she bullies this way. Any ideas?

A. Brown, Nashville

Dear A. Brown,

This letter reminds me of the Grandmother who was concerned about her Grandson biting the family dog. "He just grabs an ear and bites hard! Luckily the dog has never bitten back." I checked back with her six months later, and he had stopped the unsanitary, dangerous habit.

The two-year-old Granddaughter sounds as if she is exhibiting some nasty jealousy. She is only two and may simply need some lessons in manners.

Does this only happen when they are visiting you? Discuss this with the two sets of parents. They should let you know how they would want it handled. To punish the biter? To encourage the four-year-old to bite back?

Until they solve the problem, I would refuse to let them visit at the same time. Grandparents' role should not be the referee in a cousin battle.

Unless you have full responsibility of the discipline of these children, I feel it is the duty of the parents to handle these situations.

When a child is misbehaving in my home, I feel free to discipline lightly. If there is a major flaw in that behavior, I hand it back to the parents.

If this destructive interaction isn't stopped soon, you may be seeing the same little girls fighting over adult situations.

A lot of Grandchildren display jealousy in various ways. You can only solve these emotions when you are able to give them individualized time.

Find some activity for your strong-willed two-year-old that will bond your relationship. Select another pastime for the more passive Granddaughter. Enjoy both girls. Personalities change daily!

Henry Ward Beecher said, "That energy which makes a child hard to manage is the energy which afterward makes him a manager of life." Teaching the child to direct energy is the task!

Q: *Usually, I don't read columns about children because I am just not interested, but yours entitled "Being a Grandparent Not Always So Grand" really caught my eye. I never wanted to be a Grandmother, but was made one by a crazy young marriage of my son when I was thirty-nine. He then had two more with a second wife.*

I recently moved here from D.C., and I can't believe the way people in the South act about children. If you happen to mention you don't care to be around any children, they think you are some kind of monster. I know a lot of people who do not particularly like kids but are afraid to be honest and say so.

Children are not made to mind and have no respect for their elders. Parents don't care what they do or say, wherever they are or whenever they want. I am tired of having my meal spoiled when I am in a nice restaurant by children who are screaming or running or throwing food.

I am tired of having my vacations (that I save so hard for) spoiled by someone bringing a child along on trips that should be only for adults, and the child won't sit still or be quiet. And forget about planes; children are a real pain then and should not be allowed on them at all.

Millions are spent on schools, and they can't read, write, spell, or figure. They teach them to use all kinds of computers instead of their brains.

Well, you can see where I stand. My son was wanted and planned for, and I was older and would never have tolerated the behavior you see now from children. It is time to quit babying children and teach them some sense.

Florence, Madison

Dear Florence,

You have spoken for the "other" side of Grandparenting and let this be a warning to those who think their "cuties" are enchanting to everyone in public!

Q: My daughter called yesterday and was almost hysterical. Her twelve-year-old daughter had been to the mall with friends and had her navel pierced! I know that isn't a good thing, but she was carrying on as if her daughter had committed an act of terrorism.

I don't know how to talk to my daughter or my Granddaughter. I feel very much in the middle of this situation. Any advice?

Mabel, Granville

Dear Mabel,

I can remember when the act of one of our sons letting his hair grow long was viewed as rebellion and mutiny. My husband was more understanding and taught me to let those things pass. "One day he will be ashamed of how he looks, but there is no need to try to convince him of that today. Take several pictures and some day you will be able to laugh at yourself and shock his children."

Well, it happened just that way. Those pictures are handy and are simply mentioned when he gets on his high horse about something his (or somebody else's) children have done.

One of your Granddaughter's needs is to find out who she is, without Mom making those decisions. You and I agree this may be an unhealthy and ugly choice, but the hole will grow back. She could have done something more permanent.

Your role is to calm her mother. Can't you think of something stupid she did as a teenager? Ask her to close her eyes, remember the incident, and then realistically state how she should have handled that situation.

Your Grandparenting role is to listen without judgment and value Grandchildren for who they are. Grandchildren seem to automatically trust Grandparents—unless we let them down. You can relate some of your own experiences and how your parents handled them. Ask her how they should have dealt with you. Don't tell her tales about her parents!

Do everything in your power to help her feel she has dynamic potential just waiting to happen. Having a good outlook on their future helps young people to avoid a lot of unhealthy choices.

Franklin Roosevelt said, "We cannot always build the future for our youth, but we can build our youth for the future."

Q: *My daughter just announced that she and her husband have agreed to take their two children (seven and nine) out of public school and teach them at home. My daughter has a college degree, but not in education, and she seems very determined for the boys to have a superior education. I am concerned that she doesn't realize what she is getting into, and the boys will miss out on the social part of school. How can I feel better about this situation? How do you feel?*

B. W., Gallatin

Dear B. W.,

I am big on superior education, and I feel that no mother would undertake this immense responsibility if she weren't committed to providing an incomparable schooling environment for her child.

Your daughter has undoubtedly done research on her responsibilities and has joined a Home Education Association and registered with her local school board as to her intentions. HEA helps provide materials, advice, and encouragement. There are also local groups in most areas devoted to assisting parents of home schooled children.

Many people feel there needs to be a teaching certificate in hand to teach. This does not guarantee a person can teach!

In a perfect world, all children would be given an education designed to fit their own learning style and personality profile. Thousands of mothers instinctively know how to provide these skills. Thousands more have neither the skills nor the inclination to teach their children!

If I had my parenting days to do over, I might teach one of my sons at home. He needed a fast-paced challenge to his education and less peer pressure. The other one was geared to a regular curriculum and classroom. Looking back, I certainly see areas I could have expanded on to insure that their education was more complete.

All home-schooled children I have talked to say they get plenty of playtimes with their friends. Adam Jordan (twelve) said, "I hated going to school! Now I love to learn, and I still get to play league basketball and football with my friends after school."

Q: I am concerned that my son is pushing his four-year-old son to become an adult too quickly. They have enrolled him in violin lessons! Whatever happened to being a child? Am I not keeping up with the times?

E. C., Nashville

Dear E. C.,

For all those devoted violin people, for all those who firmly believe in starting young, for all those who will want to hang me from the nearest symphonic podium, I want to know what four-year-old understands what he is undertaking?

My mother put me in piano lessons when I was in the second grade, and I continued for ten years. It was never fun.

Children today are organized to death! Ours take piano, swimming, soccer, cheerleading, horseback riding, football camp, basketball camp, and the list goes on and on. Whatever happened to those long, hot days of summer when we enjoyed *playing*?

How many of our Grandchildren know how to play Annie Over or Red Rover or London Bridge or can count, "one potato, two potato, three potato, four?" What happened to Kick the Can? Blind Man's Bluff?

I learned to sew on a quilt in my front yard. I made clothes for my dolls with Lena Kate and Sarah May. They could sew better and taught me how to add lace to the edges. On rainy days when I had no one, I designed paper dolls and played all by myself.

Maybe we can better understand why the younger mothers do not sew. Barbie dolls come with their own elaborate attire.

We can all remember the days before television. It was a time of being creative with what life offered. How many June bugs' legs have we tied a string on? How many dirt trails have we charted for locust shells? Quilts were spread on the ground and "I See" was played with those large fluffy clouds.

No one will ever convince me our children are better off playing electronic games or rushing off to meet another pressurized schedule.

I wouldn't have missed making clay villages with Bill and Joe Davis for anything!

Q: *I am furious with my mother and will probably never speak to her again! I can't believe she would treat our wishes with such disrespect.*

We have twin girls that we are raising as vegetarians. We spent three days with my parents and left the girls with them one afternoon. She knows how we feel about meat and we had been very cautious to not eat any during our visit. She took the girls to McDonald's and fed them hamburgers!

She didn't tell us, but the children did. After I yelled and screamed, she said, "They just look too skinny. They need some meat on their little bones."

We packed up and left! I feel awful, but know I can never go back again. Do you have any suggestions to make me feel better?

Andrea, Clarksville

Dear Andrea,

Tell your mother I said: "Shame on you, Granny!"

First rule of conduct for Grandparents: Never go against parents' rules and wishes. Food requests can be related to health, religion, or personal beliefs, and you as the parent have the final pronouncement.

Now, the part that you are going to have to handle is forgiveness. First rule of parents: Forgive Grandparents for misguided love! I understand your frustrations, but I also know holding grudges will not make you feel better. You need to let go of this anger and hostility. Forgiveness can liberate you from the pain and distress.

I suggest your calmly write your mother a letter telling her why you feel the way you do about eating meat. You might send some material that explains how to eat nutritionally and remain a vegetarian. Tell her you want to have a good relationship with her, for your sake and the twins.

You are teaching many values to your children and one is to learn that people make mistakes, but forgiveness can heal. Histories seem to prove that the way we treat our parents seems to have a bearing on how our children treat us later. Think about that!

If your mother refuses to abide by your food rules, you will have to supervise them when you visit again, for I predict you will return.

Q: *My son and his wife have a new baby. This is our first Grandchild. I have smoked all of my life. My son says he is not going to allow my Granddaughter to come over until I quit smoking. This is my house!*

I think I should be able to smoke if I want to. I had already agreed not to smoke in his house, but in mine is an unreasonable ultimatum. What do you think I should say to him?

Shelby, Murfreesboro

Dear Shelby,

I can only agree with you on the point that this is your house. Statistics have shown that passive smoking (being exposed to

GRANDPARENTS' CORNER

smoke from another person's cigarette) is harmful to adults and children.

Smoke can irritate the respiratory tract of small children and make them very susceptible to infection. Wouldn't you hate to think that you caused a health problem for your new Grandbaby?

If you have ever considered discontinuing your unhealthy habit (understanding that every smoker has tried at one time or another), this is an excellent time to reevaluate your priorities. Which means more to you—your cigarettes or visiting with your Granddaughter? It is as simple as that!

READERS RESPOND TO READERS

I am responding to the Grandmother in Murfreesboro who saw no reason to stop smoking. Does that habit and that house love her, need her, and want her as much as her son and Grandbaby?

Her son not only has the right to issue her an ultimatum, he has the obligation. After a forty-four-year habit, I am now a smoke-free widow, mother, and Grandmother. We are also a bereaved family who has lost its husband, father, and Grandfather because of his smoking.

Too Late, Nashville

Your answer to Shelby in Murfreesboro was quite correct. Cigarette smoke contains more than thirty-six hundred different chemicals, and these components permeate the walls, carpets, drapes, bed covering, and overstuffed furniture.

Chuck, Joelton

I am a hair stylist and have customers who swear that they do not smoke; but when I wash their hair, the smell of smoke is so strong, I am tempted to feel they are not being truthful.

I have learned that their spouses smoke and they are receiving as much of the smoke in their bodies as the smokers are by "inhaling." Why do people continue to believe that their smoking harms no one but themselves?

Harriett, Knoxville

Q: My purpose for writing is to ask if you have any information sources about childhood obesity. My six-year-old Granddaughter has suddenly, in the past two years, put on a lot of weight. According to the pediatrician, she is in the seventy-fifth percentile and "off the chart" in weight.

She visits us occasionally (we live in the same town), but her primary food intake is at her home. We have read all the material about the food pyramid, which is helpful, but I have no idea what a serving size is for a child. Is it the same as an adult? I wouldn't think so.

I have determined not to reward her with food and not to feed between meals. I thought I could help her by letting her know what a serving is since this will be her issue to manage for the rest of her life.

Any help you can give would be appreciated.

Concerned Grandmother, Hendersonville

Dear Concerned,

After doing some research, I was shocked to discover that one out of every five children in the United States is overweight. Statistics show that obesity is caused by genetic factors, lack of physical activity, unhealthy eating patterns, or a combination of all.

You are correct in proportionate sizes. She has probably been given a caloric number to stay under. You can judge what size meat patty by looking at a calorie counter found in many places. For example, if she likes mashed potatoes, ½ cup would be much more preferable for a child than a whole cup.

You are also right in not giving rewards of food or eating between meals, but some other suggestions might be:

* Have fruit and veggies handy for snacks
* Teach her to drink water (most children don't get enough anyway)
* Get involved in physical activity—even if it is just walking around your block or through a park.

One item for all of us to remember: We are not on a diet; we are changing our eating habits to a healthier lifestyle. Now is the time to teach her a new routine.

Q: *My Grandson has moved in with his girlfriend. I think it is wrong, but haven't talked to him yet. What can I say or do to let him know how I feel?*

Crushed in Manchester

Dear Grandmother,

He already knows how you feel. You have painted a picture of your beliefs for all the years he has been around you.

As a young girl I knew right from wrong, knew what my family expected, but I still made terrible decisions.

If we look at the way some of the younger generation dress, the music they are exposed to, and the lack of morals in the media, we might like to play judge and jury for these impressionable offspring.

Every generation has their shockers! How soon we forget Frankie and Elvis? Living together seems to be the "in thing" of the last few decades.

We may think we know what is right, for experience has taught us, but condemning their actions will only drive them away.

One Grandmother shared with me their similar solution. The young couple, not ready for a wedding, agreed to unite in a Commitment Service with the entire family participating. They read 1 Corinthians:13 (those beautiful verses of love), and made vows of responsibility. Everyone in the family agreed to support their love and pray for their togetherness. That was five years ago. They were married four years ago and now have two lovely children—a family in love, working through love, to create a united love.

Love of any person says, "I love you no matter what!" not "I love you *if* you do all the things I like or believe."

Invite them over for dinner, displaying your love and commitment. Actions bellow more than wordy speeches.

Q: *I would like to comment on your advice to the Grandmother in Manchester who was concerned about her Grandson moving in with his girlfriend. You told her that experts suggest Grandparents should love Grandchildren—no matter what!*

Years ago, my sister wanted to follow a boyfriend to an out-of-state school. Our parents wanted her to stay at Vanderbilt. She asked our wonderful Grandmother what she thought about the decision, and our Grandmother told her it was "like the choice between a buckboard and a Cadillac." My sister chose Vanderbilt and she has never regretted it.

All the Grandchildren adored our Grandmother because we knew she adored us. She was able to make each and every one of us believe that we alone were her favorite. To her, we were the smartest, most beautiful, most talented, and nicest children that had ever lived and we all wanted to live up to her expectations.

Although the experts are right in their opinion that Grandparents must love their Grandchildren, it is wrong to suggest that Grandparents should not offer guidance based on their wisdom and experience.

At forty, I am completely aware that I was capable of some very bad decisions when I was twenty. I owe many of my better decisions to the fact that I chose not to please myself, but did what I knew my parents and Grandparents expected of me.

My darling Grandmother's approval was worth much more than gold to me because I already knew I had her love.

Emily, (e-mail)

Dear Emily,

What a priceless gift your Grandmother left you—the perfect role model for you. I agree that Grandparents have every right to offer advice, but the opportunity must begin when the children are small. These are the days for building trust and respect for Grandparents' opinions.

As Grandparents to small children we cannot be negative, insist on winning all the debates or expressing our philosophy at the drop of a hat. Developing relationships brings about the faith you had in your wonderful Grandmother.

Let every one of us take a lesson from your youthful wisdom.

Can't help but wonder if Vanderbilt has ever thought of using this comparison as a marketing tool?

Q: My Grandson has been living with his girlfriend for several months. Now, I find out she is pregnant. I don't know why they won't get married. He was

always such a good boy. She seems nice, but why don't her parents make her get married? We have all talked to them. I don't know what else to say.

I realize many other people go through this, but I am so ashamed.

HeartSick, Murfreesboro

Dear HeartSick,

Thousands of devoted parents and Grandparents have gone through this distressing time. You will learn to deal with the pain and the embarrassment you are feeling.

Try not to set a double standard for the girl's parents; they are dealing with the same conflict.

Four suggestions to make this circumstance turn out to be a positive misfortune:

1. The first word is *forgive* and move on to more immediate needs of the young couple. Their life is not as they had planned. Most young people dream of marriage, careers, and scheduled families. Young adults today may express their goals in a different vocabulary, but very few choose to jump headlong into parenthood and the tremendous responsibility this entails.

2. Love them with all your heart and don't let your judgment of their lives get in the way. So many of us want different lifestyles for our children, but it is *their* lives. Remember when you were young? You didn't want anyone telling you how you should or shouldn't plan your life.

3. Forget mistakes. My friend, Nancy Dean, says her mother taught her, "Try not to have to win *all* the battles with your children. Look at the overall picture."

   What is it you really want for your Grandson and your great-Grandbaby? Plan on how you can help this young couple make the most of their dilemma.

4. Most importantly—No alienation. Whatever you may think or feel, keep the channels of communication open. Breaking relationships with a relative should rarely be an option. There may come a day when it will be physically too late to repair the damage.

Q: What would you do if your Granddaughter came to you saying she was pregnant but she didn't want to tell her parents?

She has always been a good girl and her parents love her very much, but I am uncertain how they will take this news.

B. W., Mt. Juliet

Dear B. W.,

What a tremendous responsibility, but what a wonderful relationship you must have with your Granddaughter.

I hear so many Grandparents saying they feel they could handle the sexual questions of young people today so much better than their parents are obviously doing. As we get older, we feel less tension in discussing matters of chemistry, biology, and the heart.

We have seen enough cable TV not to be embarrassed, and our years remind us that sooner or later everything works itself out and life goes on.

My first question was of her age. The primary importance to that is whether she is less than eighteen years old, and whether she is in school or out on her own.

Try to relax and temporarily pretend she isn't related to you. Put yourself in her position. What would you have wanted to hear from a loving family member?

I would listen and listen and listen as long as she will talk—it may take days to give all her thoughts to you, but as she pours out her fears and anxieties, you will begin to find a way to convince her that her parents must be told.

The obvious conclusion is they are eventually going to find out.

She may need to stay with you, briefly, while the home fires settle down. She may need some counseling that you can financially afford to offer. Will she talk to a minister?

Where is the father of the baby? Is he a part of the picture? Will he talk to you?

You have been handed an extraordinary problem to deal with. By your Granddaughter's faith and trust in you, I feel confident that you can deal with this lovingly and patiently.

Go slowly and pray a lot.

Q: *I have an unusual problem. It seems backward to your regular questions. My problem is my mother—the Grandmother of my two daughters.*

Every Christmas holiday, they spend two weeks with her in Florida, where she has lived for several years. She now has a live-in boyfriend!

They are both in their seventies and this seems like such a brainless quandary, but my daughters are asking questions like, "Are they married now? You said we couldn't live with someone if we weren't married. Why are they? Do old people have sex?"

I don't have a big problem with my mother and her friend. I know Mom needs companionship and he seems to be nice from our meeting him previously.

How do I teach my children my values without condemning my mother? Should I let them go for the holidays or skip this year and hope the situation will change?

Diane, Goodlettsville

Dear Diane,

Isn't it amazing how life's questions seem to come full circle? I wonder if your mother taught you your values. Have you discussed your predicament with her? She may not want them to visit her this year.

Now is the perfect opportunity to teach your children about loving people even though we don't necessarily agree with some of their choices. Love and acceptance doesn't necessarily mean condoning a person's actions.

You can assure them older people have sex, but often live together for other reasons—finances, health, and most importantly, friendship.

Q: *I made some mistakes when I was young and I worry about my Grandchildren finding out what I did.*

I have talked with our minister and he thinks I should go ahead and tell them now. They are all teenagers and I am afraid they will lose any confidence in me they have had.

Regrets, Knoxville

Dear Grandfather,

"There is so much good in the worst of us and so much bad in the best of us, that it does not become any of us to find fault with the rest of us." I can just hear my daddy saying that about a man whom our small town had condemned for his dubious habits.

All of us have made mistakes. We have grown out of those times. We have learned and become more tolerant of other people. We should put those times behind us and live one day at a time.

I assume you have done a lot of good in those teenagers' eyes, or they wouldn't respect you so much. Tell them yourself. They will admire your courage and honesty.

I felt the need to confess some things to my Granddaughter, but she accepted the mistakes in me as she knows I would do with her.

Florence Coates said, "Thank God, a man can grow! He is not bound with earthward gaze to creep along the ground. Though his beginning be but poor and low, Thank God, a man can grow!"

Q: My Grandson recently died of AIDS. I am still in shock and don't know what to say to my friends. I don't know how he contracted this disease and am not sure I want to know.

Has any of your group encountered this and how did they handle it?

Anonymous

Dear Grandparent,

Our Real Life group has discussed many aspects of AIDS. In fact, they asked for a professional to come and give them more facts—in order to better understand the disease.

They learned there are four known ways to communicate the illness—sexual contact, sharing of injectable needles, blood transfusions (although rare since 1985 testing requirements), and pregnant mother to unborn child.

They are not sure you need to discuss this with your friends. Acknowledgment of the fact is important for your own mental health, but details seem to be unnecessary.

They presume you and your family have been able to be open with each other and deal with the emotions of death and AIDS.

We also believe you would feel better to know "how" he contacted the disease because then you can realistically deal with that situation—whatever it may be.

I have always said the Real Life group is a very broad-minded, intelligent, and caring assembly of senior citizens. They all know human beings, either in their family or friends, who are abusive drug users and realize this is an addiction that needs to be treated professionally.

Most of them are acquainted with individuals who have chosen a sexual lifestyle they do not condone, but they continue to be tolerant and loving.

An eighty-year-old widow in our group says, "I would never reject a Grandchild because he was a drug addict or homosexual or living with someone of the opposite sex. Family love may be the only way to reach them. Forgiveness is important for my own peace of mind." And this woman, who has known many problems, continues to spread kindness and devotion.

Check with your church or hospital about a support group that would give you an outlet for conversation and information.

Q: *I received the following letter from my Granddaughter who lives in Seattle, Washington. I have been so upset. She is thirteen years old and should not be feeling this way. What can I say or do for her?*

I can't wait until summer. Do you think I could come and spend a couple of months with you? I am so stressed out, I am thinking about quitting school.

Mom is always telling me about when she was in high school and said it was really like the TV shows. She said friends would meet every afternoon at a local soda shop, drink coke floats, and talk about fun stuff.

I don't have that kind of time. Between trying to figure out when everyone in a cooperative group can get together, deciding what our teacher might put on a test, and writing a paper for several classes, I am out of hours.

Mom said her summers would last forever, but I have to worry about which honors classes I can get in, in order to get in the right college, in order to be up for the best jobs.

Since kindergarten, I have heard that I was being prepared for first grade, and then each grade was a stepping-stone for starting college and facing the real world.

Nana, I am so tired.

C. M., Lebanon

Dear C. M.,

It is overwhelming to us that teenagers feel this type of anxiety. Research tells us that one-third of our teenagers are stressed on a daily basis.

Our adult world is no role model for dealing with stress. Maybe we need to back up and learn how to relax and cope with the pressures of an ever-changing environment.

Every teenager should have at least one adult in whom they can confide. Hopefully, it will be a parent, but Grandparents make a wonderful sounding board. Sometimes my Granddaughters tell me *more* than I really want to know, but I truly appreciate their trust in me.

A practical answer to your question is telling her that you would be glad to have her for several weeks. During the long summer days, you can work on her stress management and setting priorities. Take her for coke floats and picnics in the park.

Talk to her parents. They may not even realize what she is putting herself through or they may be the total cause. Changes need to be made.

Q: *I am afraid I have done something to turn my Grandson against me. Every summer he spent two or three weeks with us. He would often spend weekends when he had holidays and would beg to come more, but now he has decided not to come at all this summer.*

He just turned thirteen and I know being a teenager might have affected him. But, why would he turn away from me unless I have done something?

Elizabeth, Lawrenceburg

Dear Elizabeth,

You have evidently forgotten your feelings as a teenager. The rest of the world seemed to be from the Dark Ages and everyone else was too old to understand anything.

Their inner self wants to fight with everyone, especially parents. Grandparents usually get more respect, so the teens tend to back away. This is their way of avoiding conflict with you.

Teenage years also bring about so many changes in their disposition that you may become disenchanted with their clothes, music, mannerisms, and body decorations. This is not the time to criticize or censure their behavior. You may alienate them for life.

Continue to love from a distance and your Grandson will return when his life is less confusing.

Q: My teenage Grandson is not very talkative. Every time he is over at my house, I try every subject I can think of and he only gives me short answers.

How do I get him to talk to me?

Granny Smith, Powell

Dear Granny Smith,

Stop talking so much! Listen with him in his silence. Communication is not always verbal. Sometimes it is quiet understanding, or simply the sensitivity to know when to stay hushed. If he enjoys being in your home, it must be for some reason other than conversation.

One of these days, he will utter something profound and you will be astounded to know what he has been thinking.

Don't overpower teenagers with words; they would much rather have your love and attention.

Order pizza delivered and watch his favorite TV program with him.

Q: My husband recently had a stroke and had to go into a nursing home. He doesn't talk, yet he seems to be alert to those around him.

I am not sure whether to ask my Grandchildren to go see him or not. So far, they have avoided the issue. How do other children react to nursing homes?

Wanda, Farragut

Dear Wanda,

Two members of the Real Life group shared their experiences. Betty said, "I asked my Grandchildren to go see their Grandfather. They did and refused to go back. I told them he had changed a lot, but that he knew when they were there and still loved to hear all about their activities. They did return and have now accepted the circumstances. The younger one said, 'Gram, I sure am glad Granddad enjoyed hearing about my soccer game today.'"

The other member of the class said that her Grandchildren did go once and never went back. She didn't make or ask them to return. Several members commented their own preference would have their Grandchildren remember them as animated and lively—not in a bed.

The group suggested the easiest way for everyone in the future is to condition young children to nursing homes, before they have to face a family member in one.

Many kindergartens and scout groups go regularly and visit. When Jessica was five, she visited with her Daisy Scouts and said, "I liked sitting on the bed and singing to the old people. We played games and they laughed a lot. But, it sure did smell funny!"

The medicinal smell for young children can be startling, the lack of response from patients could be misunderstood, but if we don't prepare them for the realities in life, how will they be able to cope with their own predicaments?

Discuss this with the activity director or a nurse and ask them to help you prepare your Grandchildren.

The choice is really up to them. Do they want to visit even if there are changes in their Grandfather's personality, or do they prefer previous memories? They need to make the final decision.

Q: My father is very ill. We are wondering how to deal with his death with our children. They are five and nine years old and have spent a great deal of time with him.

Should I prepare them for the passing or wait until he is gone to try to explain his being away? Should I take them to the funeral?

B. J., Smithville

Dear B. J.,

First of all, I wouldn't wait to prepare them. Nor would I tell them it is like going to sleep. When I was little and learned, "Now I lay me down to sleep, I pray the Lord my soul to keep. If I should die before I wake, I pray the Lord my soul to take." I was scared to go to sleep.

Granddaddy did not go on a trip. They will expect him to return. Children need to learn about loss, because death is a normal process.

We all cope in individualistic styles. Some people cry, others remain emotionless, some want to talk about their loved one, others find it too difficult to talk about. Children will also react in various ways.

Describe as honestly as you can about their Grandfather. Death can often be described as a body that no longer breaths or thinks or feels. If they have experiences with the death of a pet, they can better understand a human being's fate.

Going to the funeral is a personal and individual choice for the family. Some people say it helps to deal with the reality. Others say it is too traumatic for small children. Some want to see the body. Others want to remember the living person when they were awake and smiling. If you leave the choice to the children, do not put pressure on them in any way and if they change their minds—that's OK too!

Death is such a difficult truth for any age. I would strongly suggest that you talk to your minister (if you don't have one, ask a church friend for their pastor's name) and begin to deal with the grief yourself. You may be better able to help your children if you are accepting your own loss in a healthy manner.

Again, I am all for preparation. There are so many children's books written about death. *The Tenth Good Thing About Barney*, by Judith

Viorst, is about the death of a cat and the realization that dying is merely a part of nature's cycle.

There are many with various directions leaning to your own beliefs. Ask your librarian or book store for assistance.

FINAL THOUGHTS

Reading back through these columns—some written five or six years ago—I can already find more changes that we as Grandparents must begin to make. Today, twelve-year-old children cannot get holes pierced in their body without a parent present. The teenagers must be eighteen and have identification to prove it. New problem—they borrow other people's IDs. How do we deal with these decisions as Grandparents? Do we take the ID away from them? Do we tell the parents? Do we try to reason with the teenager?

By now we should have realized that we have to handle individual personalities in various ways, but *love* is the common denominator and open-minded Grandparents should not express their shock or indignation, but listen with understanding of what it means to be a young person in today's society.

Hayden, age ten, and Audrey, age eight, are our only Grandchildren that have not hit their teen years. Tyler and Sean are now married. Stephen and Paul are in the working world. Amanda and Jessica are currently in college. These six adults have brought me into a new understanding of Grandparenting. They have grown up wondering what I was going to say in the paper about them and are now giving me advice on what to tell new Grandparents.

Whatever we face with young people, setting exemplary standards before them teaches a lifetime of beautiful character and lofty principles. My beloved Kenny, of strong character, gentle spirit, unconditional love, and unwavering compassion taught me to set perfection as a goal and reach as high as the stars. His Grandchildren saw these qualities and are motivated by them.

Enjoy your Grandchildren, but take time each day to restore your soul and enjoy the quiet waters that peacefully reside in the sphere of your imagination. Life is fleeting and we all need to stroll these last miles with a positive and joyful attitude.

Love to you all!